Vegetables

Vegetables

Judy Newton

Whitecap Books
Vancouver/Toronto

Whitecap Books
Vancouver/Toronto

Edited by Elaine Jones
Cover design and illustration by Carolyn Deby
Interior illustrations by Marji Rohla

Typeset at The Vancouver Desktop Publishing Centre Ltd.

Printed and bound in Canada by Friesen Printers, Altona, Manitoba

Canadian Cataloguing in Publication Data

Newton, Judy.
Vegetables
Includes index.

ISBN 1-895099-43-9
1. Vegetable gardening–Northwest, Pacific. I. Title.
SB324.55.N49 1991 635'.09795 c91-091069-3

In memory of my parents,
Dorothy and Merlin Newton

Contents

Preface

I have always had a deep interest in plants. As a child I wanted to be a forest ranger, but in high school I discovered that women were not allowed into the university's forestry program. Fortunately, times have changed in that respect. When I finally went to university after my family had grown up, my interests were directed more to horticulture.

For years I had a large vegetable garden, which was a source of much pleasure and satisfaction. As a novice gardener, I read everything I could find about gardening. While attending university I worked at the U.B.C. Botanical Gardens, answering the Hort Line and working part-time in the vegetable garden. The Hort Line was an education in itself. Gardeners phoned in with a wide variety of problems—from the very simplest to those that required research. Others called to tell me what varieties had worked well in their gardens and to boast about their successes. It was truly an interesting way to learn and share knowledge.

This book is designed to be easy to read and quickly provide answers to questions. It has been written for the Pacific coastal region, with its long growing season, mild winters and cooler summers. Here some vegetables can stay in the ground all winter long and the use of cold frames, cloches and other devices can extend the growing season for a wide array of other vegetables. However, the general information applies to growing vegetables anywhere in the province, and those in less temperate climates will find that adapting the information for their areas will yield surprising results. If you are new to vegetable gardening, it should give you confidence to grow most vegetables, and the experienced gardener should also find some new ideas to try in the garden.

Acknowledgments

Writing a book requires gathering a great deal of information, calling on personal experience and the resources of others. My book could not have been written without the help and support of a lot of special people.

To David Tarrant who had faith in me and who opened so many doors, thank you for all your help. And to Gerald Straley, who, with great patience, is always willing to put down what he is doing to answer my questions, thank you.

I really appreciate the help of my professors, George Eaton, Art Bomke, Bob Copeman and Murray Isman, who taught me so much, answered so many questions and gave their advice so freely.

Last, but not least, thank you to my family who put up with me while I wrote this book: Kathy and Maurice, Ken and Marji and Karen and John. A special thanks to Marji, who did the drawings twice over, and Karen, who took my photograph.

1 What Are Vegetables?

Most of us take vegetables for granted and rarely ponder the weightier subject of what a vegetable really is. Vegetables are fun to grow and they are something as children we were taught to eat. Once you start growing them you will find there is something very special about eating what you have grown yourself.

Vegetables are defined as herbaceous plants that are grown as a food. A herbaceous plant may be an annual, biennial or perennial with soft nonwoody stems, although most vegetables are treated as annuals. They may be grown for their leaves, stems, fruits, buds, roots, tubers, seeds or flowers.

This definition includes the traditional vegetables, as well as most of the plants we call herbs. Herbs are food plants that are used as flavorings and are grown in temperate areas of the world. (Just for the record, spices are usually defined as fragrant plants from tropical or semitropical countries that are used to flavor food.)

What we call "vegetables" is not a scientific grouping. Vegetables utilize various parts of a variety of plants. Location and custom dictate if a plant is grown as a vegetable or a fruit. There are, of course, muddy areas. A tomato is technically a fruit but we use it as a vegetable. On the other hand, melons and rhubarb are eaten as fruit, but we grow them with the vegetables.

As noted above, most vegetables grow for one season, but a few vegetables, such as rhubarb, Jerusalem artichoke and asparagus, are hardy perennials that die back to the ground each fall and grow again in the spring. Biennial vegetables, including Swiss chard, carrots and beets, are half-hardy but they are treated as annuals. If left to their own devices, they grow for a season, overwinter, bolt by sending up a taller flower stalk the following spring, and set seed. In the garden they are harvested in the first season and are not allowed to go to seed. Peppers, squash and melons are annuals—plants that are planted from seed, mature and go to seed all in the same season.

Vegetables that are similar are classified as a family. Within the family, different vegetables have a two-part, or binomial, botanical name. The first name is always capitalized and is the genus. The second name, which is not capitalized, is the species. If a vegetable has a particular characteristic that is different, it may be named as a variety or cultivar. For example, tomatoes belong to the Solanaceae family, their binomial name is *Lycopersicon lycopersicum*, and a cultivar that was developed to grow in colder areas is 'Siberia'.

The language of Latin is used worldwide for the botanical names of plants. Common names differ from area to area, and the same name is often applied to totally different plants. Without the Latin name it would be very confusing. In the case of vegetables it is not as important to know the botanical name: vegetables are more familiar and there aren't as many of them.

It is important for the gardener to know about vegetable families because the vegetables in a family are often susceptible to the same pests and diseases. Crops are rotated according to these family groupings, so that vegetables in the same family are not grown in the same spot on successive years.

The following families include the common vegetables.

Chenopodiaceae: includes beets, chards and spinach.

Compositae: the Daisy family, includes Jeruselem artichoke, lettuce and endive.

Cruciferae: a large genus, the brassica, cole or cabbage family, as well as radish, mustards and water cress.

Cucurbitaceae: the cucurbit or cucumber family, encompasses warm-weather vegetables such as melons, pumpkins and squash.

Leguminosae: the pea or legume family, which also includes beans.
Liliaceae: the lily family, which comprises members of the onion family—onion, garlic, leeks and shallots.
Solanaceae: the nightshade family, includes eggplant, tomato, potato and peppers.
Umbelliferae: includes plants whose flowers form umbels similar to Queen Anne's lace or cow parsnip: carrots, parsnips, parsley and dill.

All the Brassicas are not only in the same family but they are also in the same genus—for example, cauliflower and Brussels sprouts are both *Brassica oleracea.* They all smell the same and their flavors are similar, but they certainly look different.

It is thought that many vegetables were known in prehistoric times. Early humans lived in what were probably hunting and gathering societies. Once a group settled in an area, the cultivation of plants likely happened by accident—perhaps a seed, casually spit out, germinated.

History books credit women with planting the first gardens. Food plants, and later healing plants, were the domain of women, while the men hunted. Later, plants that were valuable were probably gathered in the wild and transplanted close by. Through trial and error people discovered which plants were good to eat, made them feel good, cured their pains, or even killed them. This knowledge was passed on from generation to generation. As gardens evolved, the plants were put in rows to facilitate their care, irrigation channels were dug, and water collected in pools. To protect the precious plants, enclosures were erected.

The early evidence of gardens has, for the most part, been lost because of the transient nature of plants. They live and die and do not always leave another generation. There is evidence that people gardened in 5000 B.C. because their tools remain and look not unlike the hand tools we use today. There are records of onions, leeks, melons, garlic and cucumbers in the Middle East as early as 1400 B.C. Natives of India, Persia, and South America were some of the first to grow vegetables. South America and Mexico are the home of corn, squash, tomatoes, potatoes and kidney beans. Cabbage and carrots originated in Europe.

The wild ancestors of today's vegetables are often extinct or bear little resemblance to their modern-day namesakes. Over time, vegetables have been bred for certain traits—leaf texture, early maturing, heat resistance and other desirable characteristics—but, through breeding, other characteristics have been lost. For example, the tomatoes we find in the stores during the winter have been bred so they can be harvested before they are ripe. They must have a tough skin to travel for thousands of miles without deteriorating. As a result, flavor has been lost, because the other characteristics were more important to the growers.

Efforts are now being made to collect very old varieties that may be growing wild or are still being grown in remote villages in countries where the vegetables originated. In Mexico and South America, scientists have been looking for tomatoes, corn and melons. It is important to recover these vegetables, as they often hold the key to disease and pest resistance through their genetic makeup.

For most of us, a vegetable garden does not save money but is an enjoyable and worthwhile pursuit. It's true that seeds cost very little, but when our gardens are producing, vegetables are inexpensive in the stores. What you do have is vegetables that have been grown with care, picked at their best and eaten at their freshest and most flavorful. When you grow your own vegetables, you know when and what insect and disease controls have been used in the garden. Commercial growers use more chemicals than home gardeners because as consumers we want the produce we buy to be perfect. We are all guilty of this, carefully passing over anything with a blemish. Commercial lettuce can not have even one aphid.

If you want to make the vegetable garden pay for itself, preserve the crop as it is harvested. If you live on the coast, plant crops to take advantage of our mild winter, such as spinach, leeks and winter cabbage. Make use of other methods to extend the growing season.

Growing vegetables provides a sense of accomplishment and well-being. It is great for your health as long as you can resist trying to do it all in one day. That is difficult when the weather turns mild, spring is in the air and the earth smells full of promise of good things to come. But remember, when spring comes and the gardening urge hits, not to try and do it all in one day. The most important thing to keep in mind is that growing vegetables is fun. And it is satisfying to serve home-grown vegetables for dinner: they are fresh, packed with flavor, full of wonderful nutrients and they represent many pleasant hours working or puttering in the garden.

Vegetables have many of the same basic requirements as people: food, water, warmth and light. The availability of these basic requirements determines the success of a garden. We can supply plants with water and food and even extra heat, by using cold frames and plastic covers. Changing the light is a little more difficult, but there are a few ways to increase light, and some vegetables tolerate some shade.

It is important to look at the site carefully, with all these factors in mind. Also keep in mind the existing plants. Large trees will not only shade the garden, but their roots will invade the soft rich garden soil, robbing the vegetables of water and nutrients. Some plants are even toxic to some vegetables: vegetables will not thrive near walnut, cedar or pine trees.

Light

The first priority when you decide to grow vegetables is to consider the amount of light your site gets. It is the one essential that you have least control over. The traditional site, the back corner of the yard, may not be the best spot if it is shaded most of the day by tall trees or a fence. Most vegetables require a lot of sun, a minimum of 6 to 7 hours a day—consider a farmer's field, which gets the full sun all day. But do not despair if the shady back corner is all the space you have. Leafy and root vegetables (lettuce, Swiss chard, peas, parsley, kale, turnips, carrots and bunching onions), will tolerate some shade. Vegetables that produce fruit (squash, melons, tomatoes and peppers) require full sun, but they could be grown in containers on a sunny patio.

The direction of the sun will also dictate where tall crops, such as pole beans and corn, are planted. At midsummer the sun is overhead and there is less shading, but as the taller crops gain maturity later in the summer, they can cast a shadow on smaller plants. Plant them on the north side of the garden to minimize shading. Also remember that as late summer and fall approaches the sun is not as strong and the growth of plants slows down.

There are some ways to increase the available light. If a fence or low wall shades part of your garden, paint it white to reflect the light. A clear plastic mulch or aluminum foil placed under the plants will reflect light back up to the plants.

Garden orientation is the direction you plant the rows of vegetables. Many books discuss this at great length but in a small home garden it is usually whatever works best. A north/south orientation is often recommended, but in my garden east/west works for me. If the summers are hot, the north/south orientation gives a bit of shade to each plant. This is beneficial to crops that prefer it a bit cooler, such as lettuce and other leafy vegetables. If you are planting on a slope, it is important to plant the vegetables across the slope, rather than up and down, to help prevent soil erosion.

Soil

After light, soil is the most crucial part of the vegetable garden. Soil supports the plant physically by providing a place for the roots to anchor and is a reservoir of nutrients to nourish the growing plants. Vegetables will grow after a fashion in poor soil, but the results will be discouraging.

Soils vary from place to place and even from one side of the garden to another. Soil over most of British Columbia was influenced by glaciation during the last ice age. Material was transported, eroded and deposited by the glaciers. Fifteen thousand years ago there was 5,000 feet (1,000 metres) of ice covering the Lower Mainland and about 4,000 feet (1,200 metres) covering the Interior. The glaciers scraped across the land, picking up rocks, which were later deposited as they melted. As the ice melted and the glaciers retreated, sediment was carried along by the fast-moving rivers of meltwater.

In some areas of B.C. there is only a very thin layer of soil, but in other areas, such as along the river deltas, there is a thick deposit of fertile soil. On the coast, where the forests are coniferous and the rain level is high, the soils are acidic. Soils in dryer, colder areas will tend to be more alkaline.

Soil color is not necessarily an indication of nutrient value, but is determined by the proportions of mineral and organic matter in the soil. Darker soils usually have more organic matter than lighter-colored soils. Rock, which varies from area to area in the province, physically and chemically weathers, breaking down to form the mineral content of the soil.

The mineral particles of the soil vary in size. Clay has very tiny particles, silt is a bit larger and sand varies from fine to coarse. Soils that are high in clay content will hold a lot of water and the particles bind tightly together. Sandy soils have a poor water-holding capacity because the spaces between the grains of sand are large and they cannot bind the water as the small spaces between the clays can. The mineral particles are a reservoir of nutrients for the plants. They dissolve in water and the plant is able to absorb the minerals through its roots.

The organic portion of the soil comes from dead roots, compost, and green and animal manures. High organic content improves the structure and tilth of the soil, as well as supplying the plant with nutrients. Tilth is the ease with which soil can be tilled, to ready it for planting.

The ideal garden soil is rich in nutrients, dark, friable and easily dug with a spade. Friable soil will hold its shape when moistened and lightly squeezed, but will also crumble readily. To determine the texture of your garden soil, put a small amount in the palm of your hand, add a bit of water and rub it between your fingers. If the soil feels gritty, it has a high sand content; a soapy feel indicates silt and a sticky soil that can be rolled into a long, pencil-like ribbon has a high clay content.

Topsoil

Often the urban lot contains very little topsoil, as it has been stripped off during development. One solution is to buy topsoil. Buying topsoil can be chancy, and once delivered it is hard to return if it is not suitable. Buy from a reputable dealer and inspect the soil before buying if possible.

Before you purchase topsoil, consider carefully whether this is the best solution for your garden. The soil will contain the seed of weeds that may not already be present on the property. It could contain a lot of sawdust and debris, and the particle size could be very large and need to be screened. Some topsoil is treated with a preemergence herbicide to prevent weeds from germinating; this treated soil will also stop vegetable seeds from growing.

Amending Soil with Organic Matter

Sometimes a better solution to poor soil is to amend the existing soil, rather than bringing in new soil. To amend soil, incorporate some organic matter: well-rotted compost, peat, well-rotted manure, seaweed or other organic material. Organic matter helps to hold the moisture in the soil, it contains nutrients in varying amounts, and it improves the general condition of the soil.

Organic matter also improves the soil porosity. Soil is made up of solids, air and water; the porosity is the water/air part of the soil. Plants require all three elements in balance. If the soil is soggy, the water will replace the air in the soil. Most plants will die if their roots cannot get air and, of course, they also die from lack of water.

Before soil nutrients can become available to the plants, the organic matter must be broken down by microbes. Microbes use nitrogen in the soil as their energy source to break down the organic matter. When sawdust, wood chips, or fresh manure with lots of straw is dug into the garden, the microbes use the available nitrogen, robbing the plants. To correct this problem, use extra nitrogen; it will eventually be returned to the soil after the organic matter has decomposed.

Fresh manure should only be added to the soil in the fall; it will burn tender roots if it is added in the spring. Organic matter will break down quickly in warm weather, as the microbes are more active. On the coast the organic matter will continue to break down slowly over the winter, but in colder areas the microbial activity will slow down during the winter. Rather than adding sawdust, wood chips and fresh manure directly to the garden, they can be composted first; then when added to the garden there will not be any harmful side effects.

Compost

There are whole books written on the subject of compost. It is easy to make, essentially free, and will reward you by improving the soil. The composting process generates heat, and the center of the pile will reach a temperature of 131 to 149°F (55 to 65°C). The heat will kill most weed seed and insects, and many diseases. Once the material is composted, the pile will cool down.

Compost can be made in a series of wooden bins, a chicken wire enclosure, a manufactured bin or even simply in a pile. Unless the compost is to be used for a patio or tiny garden, the purchased bins are not big enough. They are neat looking and that is a plus if they cannot be hidden away in a corner of the garden.

Compost bins are often built in a row of three: one to receive new material, the second to hold the already composting material and the third for compost that is ready to add to the garden. An average bin would be about 3 feet (90 cm) wide and deep and about 4 feet (120 cm) high. The corners should be made of sturdy, treated, 4-by-4 posts or wood that resists rotting. The sides are slats with 1-inch (2.5-cm) spaces between them. The front of the bins should have removable slats, to make it easier to remove compost. If rats are a problem, the bins can be lined with hardwear cloth (used in house construction), and a tight-fitting lid of hardwear cloth can be fashioned to cover the bin.

Chicken wire cages are easy to construct and portable. They are a great way to handle all the excess composting material in the fall. The chicken wire helps to contain the material so the wind does not blow it around. Roll the chicken wire to make an open-ended loop and stand it on end. The join may be held together with twine or wire, or you can thread a stake in through the mesh and push it into the ground. At least three stakes should be used around the cage to make it sturdy. On the coast the cage can be placed right in the garden. In the spring the material will be composted and it is easy to pull out the stakes and spread it over the garden. In colder areas it will not be ready to use in the spring, so place it in an out-of-the-way spot.

Anything that is natural may go into the compost pile—with a few restrictions. Most kitchen waste is fine. I keep an ice-cream bucket with a lid by the kitchen sink. Empty it every day or so, or it will smell. Shredded newspaper can also be composted.

Do not use cat, dog or human waste because of the risk of disease. Meat and fat should not be used because they may attract animals, although I add fish remains that I bury well. This is a bit of a contradiction, but it adds nutrients, and the red worms that fish attracts are great for the pile. If branches or corn stalks are added, shred them or cut them into small pieces first. Do not add diseased plants or weeds that have seed heads. Grass that has been treated with a herbicide should not be put in the compost for a minimum of three mowings after application.

To start the pile, put a 6-inch (15-cm) layer of vegetable matter on the bottom, then a layer of soil to supply the microbes that will break down the material. If the plants that are being added have soil on their roots, a layer of additional soil will not be needed.

There are commercial composting products available, such as 'Rot It'. As an alternative, use a high-nitrogen fertilizer, such as urea or manure. It is sprinkled between the layers to help the decomposing if there are materials that do not contain much nitrogen, such as sawdust, straw or wood chips. Instead of adding nitrogen fertilizer, materials rich in nitrogen—grass clippings, poultry manure and legumes—may be layered with the sawdust and wood chips. If you want to raise the pH, sprinkle lime on the compost. Do not add fertilizers in the same layer as lime, as the lime will cause the nitrogen to escape as a gas.

The decomposing process will not work without moisture. If the summer is dry, add water weekly. The pile should be moist but not soggy. During the heavy rainy season, cover the top with a tarp to prevent the nutrients from being leached.

The more often it is turned, the faster the material will decompose. It generally takes about six months to make compost if the pile is left to decompose on its own.

Compost is ready to use when it is crumbly and has a rich dark look. Use it as a mulch, dig it into the garden or use it in potting mixes. If it is made properly, compost will not smell, it costs nothing, and it is a sound environmental practice to recycle our waste rather than sending it to the land fill.

Green Manure

Green manure will also increase the organic matter in the soil. It is any crop that is allowed to grow for a season and is dug under before it reaches maturity. This may sound like something only farmers would do, but it is very appropriate and highly recommended for home gardeners. A green manure crop is usually broadcast-seeded, after the vegetables are harvested in the late summer or fall between, mid-August and the end of September. It is a great way to add organic material to the soil for the price of a bag of seed. You would need to haul a great deal of manure to incorporate an equivalent amount of organic material into the soil.

Green manure increases the organic matter in the soil, prevents soil erosion, moderates the soil temperature, supresses winter annual weeds and improves the fertility of the soil. Organic matter improves the physical condition of the soil by improving the soil structure, increasing aeration and water retention. The roots of the green manure crop help to hold the soil and prevent erosion from both wind and rain. The crop moderates the soil temperature from extremes. In the winter it acts as a buffer and protects the roots of plants that are growing near it. This is very helpful if it is grown between the rows of winter crops or by perennial plantings. The dense growth covers the soil, preventing winter annual weeds from growing by using the nutrients and shading them out. On the coast, where rainfall is heavy, nitrogen gets leached out of the soil over the winter; a green manure crop planted in the fall will use that nitrogen before it is leached. When the green manure is dug under, the nitrogen and other nutrients it used will be returned to the soil. It also improves the soil fertility, by bringing other nutrients closer to the surface where they will be available to the next crop. Some people cut and compost the green manure crop, rather than digging it all under.

The preferred green manure will vary from area to area, but it is usually buckwheat, legumes, fall rye or other seed mixtures. A good cover crop is spring barley (*Hordeum vulgare*). It grows quickly and then it is killed by the frost. Crimson clover (*Trifolium incarnatum*) has wonderful flowers in the spring. An annual legume, it fixes nitrogen through a symbiotic relationship with rhizobia bacteria, which converts nitrogen from the air to a form that plants are able to use. Rye grass (*Lolium multiflorum*) is a good choice for wetter soil.

There has been some concern about green manure crops turning to weeds, but as long as they are turned under in the spring that should not be a problem.

Green manure crops can be broadcast between rows of winter vegetables such as Brussels sprouts and kale. Rotate the winter garden each year, so that each part of the garden will benefit from the green manure crop.

Let the green manure crop grow as late as possible to get the most benefit. This is particularly important with legumes, because they fix most of the nitrogen in the spring. Where possible, leave it until April or later before it is dug in. It should be turned under two weeks before the vegetable crop is planted. The green manure crop can be turned under section by section or row by row, as the garden is needed, rather than turning the garden under all at once.

Soil pH

Soil pH is a measure of the acidity or alkalinity of a soil solution and it is expressed from 0 to 14 on the pH scale. The higher values are alkaline and those below 7.0 are acidic; 7.0 is neutral. Each unit on the pH scale increases or decreases by a factor of 10; that is, pH 5.0 is 10 times more acidic than a 6.0 and a 4.0 is 100 times more acidic than a pH of 6.0.

On the coast, where there is a high rainfall, the soil is acidic, or sour, and it will fall below the neutral 7 on the pH scale. Alkaline, or sweet, soils, above pH 7.0, are found in dryer areas.

Each plant has an optimum pH range. Most vegetables grow best between pH 5.2 and pH 6.8. This range is important because if the soil is too acidic, nutrients will become unavailable to the plants. For example, the more acidic the soil becomes, the tighter the phosphorus is bound to the soil in forms that are unavailable to the plants. You will be wasting your money when you fertilize.

It is easy to test your soil using kits available from nurseries. Once you have determined the pH level, you can adjust it to meet the requirements of the vegetables you are growing. To increase the pH of acidic coastal soils, add agricultural, or preferably dolomite, lime. Dolomite lime contains magnesium, which is often in short supply in coastal soils. Do not apply lime at the same time as fertilizers because the lime interacts with nitrogen and converts it into a gas that escapes into the atmosphere.

Wait a month before applying fertilizer. Lime may be applied in the early spring or fall. It moves slowly into the soil, unlike more soluble nitrogen. Lime should be dug in rather than just sprinkled on top of the soil.

Alkaline soils are acidified with the addition of acidic sphagnum moss or acidic fertilizers like ammonium sulphate, 21-0-0-24S. Lime is applied at rates of about 35 to 50 pounds to 1000 square feet (17 to 25 kg per 100 square meters). If you are a more casual gardener, that is about a good handful to the square yard or meter, sprinkled over the soil surface every three or four years.

Macronutrients

Plants require nine macronutrients—carbon, oxygen, hydrogen, nitrogen, phosphorus, potassium, sulfur, calcium and magnesium—in fairly large quantities.

Carbon and oxygen enter the plant through the leaves from the air and are important in photosynthesis. Hydrogen enters the plant through the roots as a component of water and is essential for chemical reactions within the plant.

Nitrogen is part of all plant cells and is required for green growth. Too much nitrogen results in leaves that are large, lush and susceptible to disease and pests. Excess nitrogen reduces the amount of fruit, seed and storage root, and also reduces winter hardiness. Too little nitrogen stunts the plant, and the leaves will be small and yellow or light green. Nitrogen is removed from the soil by the growing crop, leaching and erosion.

Phosphorus is needed by the seedling when cell growth is rapid in the spring. It stimulates root development and is necessary for flower and seed formation. Phosphorus deficiency symptoms are purplish leaves, stunted growth and reduced yields of fruit and seed. Phosphorus is rarely leached unless it is in the soil in excess. In the Fraser Valley, where it has been put on the fields in large quantities, it has leached into the ground water. Phosphorus is removed by the crop and it can be converted to an unavailable form in the soil; very acid, dry or cold soil lessens its availability. Phosphorus deficiency may show up in crops early in the spring when the soil is cold.

Potassium is used for starch and sugar formation. Plants store energy as sugar or starch and these are often the parts of the plants that we harvest. For instance, potato tubers contain starch and sweet potatoes contain sugar. Potassium promotes disease resistance and winter hardiness, and is important in the formation of fruit. Lack of potassium will cause reduced yield, curling and mottling of the older leaves and poor root growth.

Calcium, magnesium and sulfur are used in smaller amounts than nitrogen, phosphorus and potassium, but they are now considered macronutrients because the plant uses them in larger amounts than the micronutrients. Calcium is important for cell division and early plant growth. Calcium deficiency deforms the top, or terminal, growth. Some plants get black spots or turn black. Lack of calcium also plays a role in blossom end rot, a disease of tomatoes. Magnesium is part of the chlorophyl molecule and a deficiency shows up as interveinal chlorosis (the leaf surface between the veins turns yellow) on older leaves. Sulfur is needed for root development and a deficiency causes reduced growth and light green leaves.

Micronutrients

Micronutrients are nutrients that are needed in small amounts. They are iron, copper, chlorine, boron, manganese, molybdenum and zinc. Some, like boron, manganese and copper, are toxic to plants in large amounts.

Fertilizers

The soil will already contain nutrients in varying amounts, and additional nutrients are supplied by fertilizers. The macronutrients are usually added to the soil through chemical and organic fertilizers. The micronutrients are usually available in the soil, although they are sometimes in short supply or they may be there but unavailable to the plants. Nutrients are bound together in the soil with other nutrients.

Most plants need many different nutrients to grow, but during certain times in the growing season a plant will use more of one nutrient than another. For instance, nitrogen is needed in the largest amount when the plant is actively growing. In the spring plants need extra nitrogen to make leaves and other green parts. Later in the summer, when the plant is setting seed or setting fruit, it will use more phosphorus and potassium. The science of soil is a complicated one. Nutrient deficiencies are often difficult to detect, as the symptoms often overlap, and the diagnosis is inconclusive.

Packaged fertilizers list three numbers, such as 6-8-6, which represent the concentrations of the three main nutrients. The first number represents nitrogen (N), the second phosphorus (P), and the third potassium (K). The rest of the content of the fertilizer bag may be other nutrients and a filler.

Granular fertilizer is applied in several different ways. It can be broadcast over the whole surface, or incorporated into the top 2 to 4 inches (5 to 10 cm) of soil. Banding places the fertilizer 2 inches (5 cm) to the side and below the soil surface where the plant or seed will grow. Side-dressing places the fertilizer to the side of established plants. Each method has its uses and cautions. Broadcasting may be used along the row where seed has been sown but do not do the whole garden, as the area between the rows does not need to be fertilized. Banding places the fertilizer in the root zone, and it can be a problem if the tender new roots come in contact with the fertilizer and are burned. Side-dressing is usually applied to established crops or used when transplants are planted. Do not put the fertilizer against the stem or onto the leaves as they may be burned by the fertilizer.

Liquid fertilizer is usually used after the plants are growing or when plants are transplanted. The nutrients are more readily available to the plants in liquid form.

There is a long list of organic fertilizers, including manure, peat, compost, seaweed, fish fertilizer, blood meal, bone meal, urea and organic wastes from processing plants. Bulky organic materials, such as manure, peat and composts, will supply some nutrients, but they are used mainly to improve the tilth of the soil. Organic materials supply energy for microorganisms. Except for fresh manure, they will not burn the roots of plants.

A disadvantage of organic fertilizers is that most are low in nutrients. Used alone, they will not supply all the nutrients that plants need. Not all manure is the same; its nutrient content will vary depending on the type of animal it came from and what the animal has eaten. If organic fertilizer is readily available it is fine to add to the garden, but for the city gardener it may be too expensive for the return. Instead, a city gardener can use green manures and make compost to supply the organic matter for their garden.

Correcting Deficiencies

Nitrogen deficiencies often show up later in the season if the plants have used up the fertilizer that was put down in the spring. To correct, give the plants a balanced fertilizer like 6-8-6. This is the formula I use when I plant the garden and for topdressing during the growing season. Urea (incorporated into the top 3 inches/8 cm of soil to minimize the loss of nitrogen to the air), manures, organic material, and legumes will also supply nitrogen to the soil.

Phosphorus deficiency is corrected easily with some super phosphate (0-20-0) fertilizer. Bone meal and animal manures contain phosphorus.

Potassium deficiency can be corrected with potassium sulfate, muriate of potash and potassium chloride, all sources of potassium.

Calcium carbonate is a good source of **calcium**. Calcium is also supplied to the soil in lime. If dolomite lime is used it contains **magnesium** as well, or you can use magnesium sulfate (Epsom salts). **Sulfur** is contained in combination with other fertilizers, in elemental sulfur or superphosphate, and is released as organic matter decomposes.

Micronutrients are available for sale as trace elements, or they are included with other fertilizers. Read the fine print on the fertilizer package to see what is included.

Soil Testing

Soil samples can be tested at soil laboratories, which are listed in the yellow pages of the telephone directory under Laboratories-Testing. The soil test will include the status of the main plant nutrients, pH and salinity, as well as recommendations for the amount and type of fertilizer to apply to the soil.

To collect the soil sample, take about ten random samplings from the area. With a shovel or trowel, dig a hole about 8 inches (20 cm) in depth. Take a slice of the soil from the side of each hole and place it in a clean bucket. Mix up the collected soil and break up any lumps. Remove about 1 pound (.5 km), spread out the soil on a paper and let it dry before sending it to the lab. Note any problems, such as high water table. If there is a particular problem in one part of the garden, collect a separate sample for that area.

Dealing with soil and plant nutrition may seem like a bit of a mystery, but with experience it becomes easier. As the soil is improved by adding compost and other organic material, it will become a pleasure to dig and the plants will benefit from soil that is easily penetrated by the roots.

Air

Air movement is important to healthy vegetables. An open garden allows cold air to drain out and good air circulation reduces disease problems. Wind is a cooling and drying force, and can be both good and bad in a garden. A slight breeze will dry leaves, making them less susceptible to disease, but a strong wind will erode soil and remove a lot of moisture from the plant through transpiration—loss of water from the leaves into the air. In spring the winds help to dry the soil, making it ready for planting.

If the garden is subject to strong winds, a hedge might be planted on the side of the prevailing winds. A fence will also act as a break, but if it solid, the winds will swirl over it.

3 Planning and Planting

Planning and planting are some of the most exciting aspects of having a vegetable garden. In the winter, when there is not too much that can be done in the garden, I pore over the seed catalogues as they start to arrive. I get out my record book and plan where each vegetable will be planted. Then, with the first whiff of warm weather, it is hard not to be impatient about getting out into the garden. There is usually plenty to do without stepping in the wet soil: pruning, tidying, sorting out pots and seed flats. The most important thing to remember is to hold back on planting. A few warm days does not mean that the cold weather is over. Be patient!

If this is your first garden, think small when you make your plans. Remember the old saying, "your eyes are bigger than your stomach." Vegetable gardens are a bit like that. In the spring, when everything is planted, it looks great, but vegetables need a lot of care. The beds need watering, weeding and fertilizing, and the produce must be picked and preserved. The weeds will grow faster than the vegetables in the spring, and there is nothing more discouraging than weeds that get ahead of you. If you find that the garden is too small, it can be enlarged next year.

When you are planning, remember that there is no law that says that vegetables have to be planted in a separate area of the yard. It wasn't until the time of Pliny the Younger (62-116 A.D.), that the Romans separated their plants by how they were used. Many vegetables are very ornamental and can be interspersed with other plants in the flower garden. Tuck a pretty 'Red Sails' lettuce, a few radish and some spring onions in between the annuals; they will be harvested before the flowers get too large. Ornamental corn, curly kale, strawberry chard, most herbs and asparagus are all perfect in a flower bed. The asparagus will be harvested before the perennials have put on much growth and the fernlike foliage is a nice foil for the flowers. Scarlet runner beans serve a dual purpose if you plant them as a screen. Their bright red flowers are lovely and the beans are tasty.

Where to Buy Seeds and Plants

Seeds are available from several sources: catalogues, seed racks at garden centers, garden specialty stores and even the local grocery store.

The seed catalogues are out in December or January, and it is never too soon to place your order. (See Sources, at the back of this book, for seed companies.) If you order seeds, you will often have a better choice than buying seeds from racks. The catalogues usually have more information about the seed than is printed on the seed package, and it is easier to plan at home from catalogues.

If you prefer, buy your seeds from a reliable nursery or garden shop that carries fresh seed. Try to shop from a list, but be flexible and try new varieties that catch your eye. The seed in local stores will often be more suitable for your area, whereas a seed catalogue may cater to the whole country. Seeds sold locally are a good source for extra seeds, especially if you have run out of those that are sown frequently, like radishes.

It is convenient to buy seeds in grocery stores, but they may have a limited choice.

Transplants can be grown from seed at home, which is the most economical way of doing it. They are sold at garden centers and grocery stores in the spring. The choice of varieties is limited, and in many cases the variety of the vegetable is not specified.

When you are purchasing transplants, look for healthy plants: the roots should not be growing through the drainage holes, the leaves should not be yellow, the plants should be compact and they should not be wilted. Be wary of buying any of the brassicas unless you are buying them from a reliable source—they could be infected with club root. Once club root is in your soil, it is essentially there forever.

Transplants are a real plus if you have a small garden. If you only need one tomato or six lettuce plants, it often makes sense to buy them.

Records

Keep a record of what you plant and where. It does not need to be fancy, but it is an essential reference as the garden matures. Enter varieties you have grown, where they were planted, and how they performed. Did the insects dine on it? Did it bolt? Was the flavor good? Did the family eat it? What was the weather like? Give a variety more than one chance: it might have a bad year and yet it will perform well most years. Keep a record of where you grow different types of vegetables, so you can rotate the crops each year.

Crop Rotation

Crops should be rotated each year because different plants use varying amounts of nutrients and harbor different pests and diseases. Plants also react differently to manure and lime. Root crops, such as carrots, will have many hairy roots if there is too much manure in the soil and potatoes should not be grown where the soil has been limed: a more acidic soil will help to control scab disease. The cabbage family grow better when the soil is less acidic, and they are grown in the part of the garden where lime has been added.

Plants are usually divided into three basic groups for crop rotation: the root crops, the brassicas (cabbage family), and everything else. These groups are not meant to be strictly adhered to, but they will give you a starting point for arranging the vegetables in the garden.

Root Crop	Brassica	Other
beets	broccoli	beans
carrots	Brussels sprouts	celery
parsnip	cabbage	leeks

Root Crop	Brassica	Other
potato	cauliflower	lettuce
	kohlrabi	onion
	radish	peas
	turnip	peppers
	kale	spinach
		squash family
		corn
		tomato
		Swiss chard

Draw a plan of the garden, dividing it into three (or four—if you want a section for perennial vegetables) plots for the three different groups of vegetables and the three soil-amending materials: manure, other organic material and lime. Dig manure into one-third of the garden; here you will grow any of the plants listed under "other." If the soil is acidic, lime is added to the second third of the garden; the cabbage family is grown here. The third part is amended with organic material, such as compost, seaweed or leaf mold; root crops are grown in this section.

In the second year, rotate the crops and the amending material. Last year's manured area will receive compost and root crops will be grown there. In the third year add lime and grow the cabbage family. By rotating the garden this way, each vegetable will have the best growing conditions and no area of the garden will be depleted of nutrients. Remember, though, that these are not hard and fast rules: you can tuck some lettuce plants between the cauliflowers and nothing terrible will happen.

Year 1	manure other	lime brassica	compost root
Year 2	compost root	manure other	lime brassica
Year 3	lime brassica	compost root	manure other

Perennial vegetables—rhubarb, asparagus and Jerusalem artichokes—should be planted in a separate bed or an area to one side, because this bed will not be dug and planted each year. When perennials are divided, rotate them to a new bed if possible.

When to Dig

Ideally the vegetable garden should be dug in the fall, leaving rough chunks of soil to break down over the winter from the action of frost and rain. This will improve the tilth of the soil, as well as expose insect eggs to the birds. In the spring, when the ground has dried out enough to be dug easily, the soil is turned and raked to make a smooth bed suitable for planting.

When to Plant

All plants have a minimum temperature below which they will not grow. Gardeners tend to ignore this, especially when spring awakens the gardening urge. People often put in the whole garden on the first warm day, when the soil is still wet and cold. Then they wonder why the seeds don't germinate or the plants don't survive. This principle also applies to winter vegetables; if they are planted too late in the fall, they do not have time to put on the necessary growth before winter sets in.

On the coast it is possible to have a winter garden. Plant it for easy access, as the soil will be wet and will become compacted if it is walked on. Permanent pathways will alleviate the problem.

Vegetables are divided into two groups, warm- and cool- season crops. The plant's place of origin is usually a clue to which group it falls into. Cool-season crops grow better when the temperatures are not too hot—around 50 to 60°F (10 to 15°C)—and they are grown for their vegetative parts, the stems and leaves. These plants originated in Europe, parts of Asia and North America. Some cool-season vegetables are peas, radish, asparagus, parsnip, broad beans and beets. Half-hardy crops that will withstand some frost are spinach, curly kale, Swiss chard, Brussels sprouts, and onions. These plants are started during the summer and are harvested through the fall and winter until a severe freeze kills them. Curly kale and spinach will survive even severe frosts.

Warm-weather vegetables are grown for their fruit. They come from

South America, Mexico, Africa and parts of Asia and can not be planted out or seeded until the nights are warm, 55 to 60°F (13 to 18°C). Some examples are tomatoes, peppers, eggplants, most beans, corn, melons and squash.

When temperatures drop below a plant's minimum requirements, it will remain static, showing no new growth. If it is cold, the plants will die. Warm-weather crops will die or be permanently set back if the temperature drops too low, even though it may not be below freezing.

Most vegetables have varieties that have been developed to be hardier than others. Choose these if your garden is cold, or if the plants are to be harvested into the winter.

The seed catalogues list the number of days to harvest or maturity for many varieties of seed. The figures are only a guideline. The catalogues usually service the whole country so the numbers will vary from region to region and from season to season. For instance summer weather on the coast is cooler than in the Interior, which means it may take a particular variety longer to reach maturity here than in the Interior.

A catalogue might list an early tomato, 'Sub Artic Maxi', at 48 days and a 'Yellow Stuffer' at 80 days. If the last frost in your area is on July 6th and the first frost is August 30, there are only 56 growing days, and during that time some of the days may be too cool for growth. You would probably do better with the 'Sub Artic Maxi'. However, some years the growing season will be longer, and it does not hurt to try different varieties to see how they will perform in your garden.

A low area in a garden can often be a frost pocket. Cold air is heavy and it will settle there. If you have low areas in your garden, grow the hardiest plants there, or wait longer in the spring before planting it. A warm, south-facing slope will be ideal for some warm-weather crops.

Temperature is all-important, but gardeners don't have to wait until nature warms the soil in some cases. Temperatures can be raised by using a cold frame or by covering plants with plastic tunnels, cloches or plastic mulch. For centuries the French used large, glass bell jars in their gardens. The bottomless, bell-shaped jars acted like small greenhouses over each tender plant. Today we use clear plastic cloches. You can purchase many variations or make your own. Coverings will allow you to plant a crop earlier and it may be possible to harvest over a longer period of time, allowing those who live in colder areas to grow tender crops.

Another technique is to use raised beds, which heat up faster than flat beds in the spring. They can be made out of wood, bricks or stone.

Chapter five has detailed information on extending the season, including temporary covers, cold frames, raised beds and mulches.

Direct Sowing

Many vegetable crops are directly sown in the ground. These are crops that do not transplant well, such as the root crops, peas and beans. Direct sowing does not take up indoor space or require the labor that growing transplants entails.

To prepare the soil, rake it smooth and level it. This is important, as seeds must be touching the soil to germinate. If there are lumps, the seeds can fall between the cracks in the soil and may not germinate. The particulars for each vegetable are in the encyclopedia section under each entry.

Vegetables can be planted in single rows, double rows or in bands. Each has its merits. Single rows, with a path between each row, take up a lot of space, but for large plants like cabbage and cauliflower this method works well. Planting in back-to-back rows or in blocks of rows is a better use of space, and works well for smaller vegetables like lettuce and onions. A block of rows must not be any wider than is comfortable to weed; you must be able to reach the middle of the rows from each side.

Not only is space saved when plants are grown in blocks or double rows, there will be less compaction of the soil with the reduced number of paths. To make even better use of the space, stagger the plants in multiple rows.

```
x           x           x           x
      x           x           x           x
x           x           x           x
      x           x           x           x
```

You can also scatter the seeds within a block, instead of planting them in rows, but there is less control of the planting this way. You may find that the seeds are clumped in one area and are too thin in others.

Seeds are always planted at greater densities than you will want once the plants have germinated and are growing. This may seem wasteful at first, but seeds are relatively inexpensive. If they were sown at the correct spacing there would be many gaps in the row, as only 60 to 80 percent of the seeds will germinate. Of those that do germinate, some seedlings will die from disease and others will fall prey to the hungry slug and other pests.

Thinnings are not always wasted. In some cases they can be transplanted into a bare spot somewhere else or they may be tossed into the evening salad.

Transplants

Transplants are plants that have been started from seed indoors or outdoors and then planted into the garden later. Vegetables that need a longer growing season, such as tomatoes, melons and peppers, are started this way. Most vegetables may be grown as transplants, but some are more difficult to transplant, especially the root crops. They have a tap root (a long, single root) and if the tip is broken the root will split as it grows. They are usually seeded direct due to the difficulty of transplanting. Lettuce and the brassicas transplant easily and are grown either way. The advantages of using transplants are that the plants will all be a uniform size and the crop will be harvested earlier. As noted above, it is necessary in some cases, so that the crop will have the extra growing time it needs to reach maturity.

Seeds should be started in a growing medium that will not hold too much water. A good mix is sand, vermiculite, sphagnum moss or a mix with 1/3 perlite, 1/3 peat or sphagnum, and 1/3 vermiculite or sand. Potting mix is not necessary, because the germinating seedling does not need food immediately, using the nutrients stored in the seed.

Flats, or plastic, clay or peat pots, cottage cheese containers or cut-off milk cartons can all be used to start seedlings. Individual peat pellets, pots or blocks of peat cells are great, but peat is very hard to recharge with water so do not let them dry out. Newspaper placed in the bottom of the flat or pot will hold the soil in. Small seeds are barely covered with soil; the larger the seed, the deeper it is planted–up to 1/2 inch (1 cm) deep.

After sowing the seeds, cover the seed flat with plastic until the seeds germinate. You can also use newspaper to cover the flats, but I find the soil dries out too quickly. At the Plant Science Greenhouse at UBC, they water the seed flats with a fungicide after sowing.

Place the pots or flats in a warm place until the seeds germinate. If you have a small number of seeds, you can use the top of your refrigerator.

The average soil temperature required for germination of vegetable seeds is from 75 to 85°F (22 to 27°C). Some vegetables, such as lettuce, celery and peas, germinate best when the soil temperatures are lower. The warm-weather crops, tomatoes, peppers and melons, need warmer temperatures. The closer to the optimum temperature the soil is, the shorter the germination period.

Until the seeds germinate, from a few days to several weeks on average, they do not need to be in the sun or under grow lights. Check the pots or flats frequently to see if the seeds have germinated and to see that no fungus is growing in the flats.

Once the plants have developed their first true leaves, it is time to transplant them into flats or pots that contain a richer soil. The first pair of leaves to emerge are the seed leaves, which are often a different shape from the true leaves. The second pair of leaves are true leaves.

By now the seedlings will have used up the reserve in the seed. Use a basic potting mix of 1/3 peat, 1/3 perlite, 1/3 soil. Once seedlings have true leaves they can be fertilized. Use a liquid fertilizer like 20-20-20 at half-strength every two weeks, starting two weeks after transplanting.

Seedlings require a lot of light. If you are growing a lot of transplants inside, you'll need artificial lights because you'll run out of window sills. Place the seedlings as close to the light as they can get without actually touching it. As the seedlings grow you will need to gradually lower the plants or raise the lights. If the lights are hung with a chain it is easy to adjust. If the light unit is fixed, raise the pots by setting them on other pots turned upside down or on a box.

Transplants must be hardened off before they are put into the garden. Hardening off simply means getting the seedlings gradually accustomed to the outdoor environment with its air, wind, and sun. Start by putting the plants outside in a sheltered, shady spot for a few hours each day, gradually increasing the time and the exposure to the sun. Flats of transplants can be placed in a cold frame several weeks before it is safe to plant them in the garden. By the time the garden is warm enough, the plants will be hardened off and be ready to be transplanted.

When planting out the seedlings, disturb the roots as little as possible and plant them far enough apart to accommodate the mature plant. Transplant on an overcast day or in the evening. The seedlings must be shaded from the sun for several days. Use a board stuck in the ground or a cut-off milk carton (open at both ends) to shade each transplant. The milk cartons fold flat for storage and can be used for many years.

Interplanting

Faster-maturing vegetables, such as lettuce, radishes, early beets and spinach, may be interplanted between other plants that take a longer time to grow, such as Brussels sprouts or cabbages. The faster-growing plant will be harvested before the space is needed. The natives of Mexico and South America planted beans to climb the corn plants and squash to grow beneath them, utilizing the whole growing area. If it is hot where you garden, plant spinach and lettuce in the shade of the pole beans, peas or corn.

Succession Planting

Succession planting is good garden management; as one crop is harvested another is planted. When the early cabbage, lettuce and spinach are harvested, it is time to plant late cabbage varieties, Brussels sprouts and the warm-weather crops. It does not have to involve a whole row. When a vegetable is harvested, have some transplants ready to tuck in the spaces or sow a few seeds.

Companion Planting

Companion planting means growing different plants together, such as carrots and onions. Each gives off an odor, which is thought to discourage the other plant's pests–in this case, the carrot rust fly and the onion maggot. Marigolds are also reported to deter insects. I plant them around the garden, just in case, and they are pretty! There is no scientific proof that companion planting works, but if a combination works for you, it makes sense to use it.

Pregerminated Seeds

This method is used primarily with beans, corn, squash, melons and peas which have large seeds. Place the seeds between sheets of damp paper towel in a plastic bag and put the bag in a warm place. The advantage of pregermination is that you will know that the seed is viable and will germinate. It also gives you a head start, as the soil can be cool when you plant the germinated seed. Check the seeds each day as they will germinate quickly. Once the root is showing, plant the seed into the garden. Handle them carefully; the root is fragile.

Fluid Gel Sowing

Gardeners who are looking for something new to try might have some fun with fluid gel sowing. It is a technique used by commercial growers who need to have an even stand in their fields to make a crop pay and for easy harvesting. Seeds sown in fluid gel are already germinated, so that each plant grows at about the same rate. It also ensures that there will not be spaces in the row where the seeds have not germinated. This is a technique to try experimentally as it is time-consuming on a small scale.

Fluid gel seeding works best with small seeds, like lettuce, onions and spinach, which would normally be planted in rows. The seeds must be pregerminated, then mixed with a gel and piped into the seed row.

To germinate the seeds, spread a couple of layers of dampened paper towels onto a cake pan or tray and spread out the seeds. Cover them with another damp paper towel and put the whole thing into a plastic bag in a warm place. You can use the top of the refrigerator or a heating pad turned on low. Watch the seeds carefully; they are ready to sow as soon as the root is barely showing (it will be just a bump). If the root has already emerged, the seeds have been left too long and the root will break off as it is squeezed out of the bag. If any seeds have not germinated, throw them out.

Make the gel with cornstarch and water. (Wallpaper paste can also be used, but read the fine print first to be sure it does not have unwanted additives like fungicides or other chemicals.) Cornstarch is prepared by gradually adding 1 cup (500 ml) of cold water to 1 tablespoon (15 ml) of corn starch. Heat and stir the mixture on the stove until it thickens, then cool. Once cooled, the mixture will have a consistency like soft jelly. It will take a bit of practice to get the consistency just right. Gently stir in the seeds and fill a pastry bag or a sturdy plastic bag with the mixture. Fill the bag and cut off the bottom corner if using a plastic bag. Start with a small hole and enlarge it if the gel is not flowing out smoothly. Lay out lines of gel according to your garden plan, and cover the gel and seeds with soil to the correct depth for that particular vegetable.

With this method the seeds need to be planted when they are ready. If it is raining heavily or you have a busy week and you can't get into the garden, they may be stored for several days in the refrigerator if necessary. Try some of the smaller seeds, particularly ones that have spotty germination. You can also try fluid-sowing peas and other seeds mentioned under pregermination; although the seeds are larger, they are easy to handle. As you become more proficient, you can experiment with some of the others.

Watering

Watering a garden may seem simple and straightforward, but it is not as easy as it seems. Probably the most common problem is underwatering. Sprinkling the garden every day may not be sufficient if you are only wetting the surface. The roots of some plants go deep into the soil and may become starved for moisture if the water has not penetrated enough. After you water, check to see how far down the soil is wet. It is better to water less frequently but more thoroughly each time.

I bury a plastic bottle (bleach, large soft drink or milk bottle) beside large vegetables like the squashes. Cut the bottom out and make a hole in the cap. Bury it upside-down. It is easy to fill with water, which slowly leaks through the hole in the cap into the soil near the root zone.

If water is restricted, dig a small trench around the plants; it will form a basin to hold water around that plant rather than watering the whole area. Consider soaker hoses or water trickle systems that only wet the soil. Evaporation is less than if you use a sprinkler, a real water saving. Plants will also be less prone to disease if the foliage is kept dry. If you must use a sprinkler system, water during the morning to give the leaves a chance to dry before night.

Do not waste water in the garden. Set sprinklers so they water the area intended and not the driveway or sidewalk. If you live where there are water shortages, gray water—bath or laundry water—can be used to water the garden. The soap in the water will not harm the plants. Use fresh water every third watering or so, to help leach the additives in the gray water.

If they don't get enough water, some plants will wilt during the heat of the day; as the temperature cools the leaves will look fine again. In most cases this is very hard on the plants. Even if they do not die once they have wilted they will not fully recover. Pumpkins and cucumbers are exceptions. This family will wilt even if the water is sufficient. It is a trait of the family, which helps them to conserve moisture.

Some crops, such as cabbage, cauliflower, corn, cucumbers, squash, onions and peppers, will tolerate a broad range of water availability. Lettuce, beets and peas have medium requirements for water, but celery must always have what is called field capacity of water. Field capacity is defined as the amount of water left in the soil two to three days after it has been saturated. Ideally, the soil will still be damp, but this does not mean the plants should be in soggy soil that does not drain well.

The type of soil in your garden determines how well the water is retained. Sandy soils do not hold the water and it will drain through very quickly. Loamy soils will hold moisture because of their organic content. Clay soils hold water and are slow to dry out in the spring, making it hard to get onto them to plant. The ideal garden soil is friable, loamy soil.

You will soon learn the requirements of your own garden based on the type of vegetables you grow, type of soil and weather. The longer you garden, the better you will be at judging the amount of water the garden needs.

4 Vegetables in Containers

If you haven't the space in your yard for a vegetable garden, containers can be the ideal solution. There are several advantages to growing plants in containers, which can be anything from an empty cottage cheese container to a beautiful Italian clay pot. They vary from those small enough to sit on a window sill to very large ones that would take a fork-lift truck to move. In many cases, containers can be moved around to take advantage of the sun or shade. They can also be raised, so that anyone can garden, even if they are unable to bend down to the ground. The soil in containers heats up faster than the soil in the ground, making container gardening ideal for peppers, squash and eggplant. If the garden soil has a disease like club root, you can grow the cabbage family in a container with new soil.

Container-grown vegetables are fun to grow, do not require a lot of space and rarely need weeding. Since they dry out easily it is hard to leave them for a few days, but mulching minimizes the problem. You may also be able to move the containers to a shady spot for a few days while you are away, to reduce water loss.

Vegetables Suitable for Container Growing

All vegetables can be grown in containers—even tall plants like corn if the container is the size of a half barrel. More usual are the smaller varieties of vegetables, including bush varieties of squash and tomatoes, either staked or allowed to range over the side of the container. Carrots may be grown in pots, but choose varieties that have short roots. The only vegetables that will not do well in containers are varieties such as 'Atlantic Giant Pumpkins'. Perennial asparagus and rhubarb grow well year after year in containers. Peas or beans grown on a trellis either secured to the container or on a wall behind it will be thick enough to provide privacy between balconies or patios. In the fall when more light is desirable and it is too cool to sit outside the vegetable screen dies back.

Many vegetables are very attractive in their own right and they can be mixed with flowers in the containers. If you have really limited space, or if you just like the way they look, plant a hanging basket with vegetables and herbs. Cherry-type tomatoes, different kinds of lettuce, little green onions, herbs and Swiss chard are good choices. Vegetables that are harvested leaf by leaf are appropriate for all containers and a good choice for small families. Swiss chard, kale and leaf lettuce are a few of the vegetables harvested this way.

Container Size

To successfully grow vegetables, the minimum size of the container is 12 by 12 inches (30 by 30 cm) or preferably 18 by 18 inches (45 by 45 cm). This does not mean that a pot that is smaller will not work, but it will dry out quickly and does not allow much room for roots. Use smaller containers for a single lettuce plant or leaf lettuce, a few green onions or a few radishes. Tall plants, which can be blown over by the wind, need a larger container. (Sand in the potting mix will also add weight to the pot.) Half barrels are great for growing vegetables; scarlet runner beans or other climbers are wonderful in the barrels.

Soil, Watering and Fertilizing

The guidelines for watering, drainage and good soil in vegetable gardens apply to container gardening. Soil can be purchased for containers or it may be mixed, using 1/3 topsoil, purchased soil or pasteurized, loamy garden soil, 1/3 peat moss, and 1/3 perlite. To make the absorption of water easier, moisten the peat moss with warm water before mixing. Dampen the perlite before it is poured to reduce the dust. Coarse builders' sand may be used instead of perlite.

For each bushel (30 quarts/35 liters) of soil, mix in 4 ounces (120 g) of dolomite lime and 6 ounces (180 g) of Osmocote or Nutricote slow-release fertilizer, or 4 ounces (120 g) of granular 6-8-6 fertilizer.

I use a garbage bag to mix soil in, if I am working where it is not convenient to do it on a driveway or other paved surface. To mix large amounts of soil, dump the various ingredients onto the floor and shovel the pile over to another spot, making a new pile. After you do this three times, the pile will be well mixed. I store extra mixed soil in a clean garbage can with a lid.

Pasteurized soil is also called sterilized soil. It is not really sterilized, because if it was heated high enough to be sterilized, everything would be killed, including the beneficial bacteria. The pasteurizing process kills most weed seeds, disease and insects.

You can pasteurize the soil yourself, although you should be warned that damp soil cooking does not smell like chocolate cake. To minimize the effects of the smell, use the barbecue instead of the oven or microwave. Place the damp soil in a roaster pan and cover it with tin foil. Insert a meat thermometer into the center and heat it until it reaches 180°F (82°C). If an oven is used set it at 200°F (93°C) for about half an hour. Microwave the soil, in a covered microwave-safe dish, on a medium setting. Use a meat thermometer and check the soil at 5-minute intervals. It is important not to overheat the soil or the beneficial bacteria will be destroyed.

Each year the soil in containers should be amended with fresh soil, compost or well-aged manure. For large containers, replace one-third of the soil or top it up with compost. Smaller containers should have the soil completely replaced each year.

One of the major drawbacks to container growing is the need for frequent watering. The smaller the container, the faster it will dry out; during really hot weather plants may have to be watered twice a day. If the soil is allowed to dry out, plants like cucumbers and lettuce will be bitter, and tomatoes will develop blossom end rot if the soil moisture fluctuates too much.

There are several techniques for dealing with rapid drying. To slow down water loss from the soil, mulch the top of the container with moss, seaweed, plastic or newspaper. Moss looks great and it is easy to find in the spring on the coast. Plastic bottles with a hole punched into them can be placed in the soil and filled with water to drip slowly. The size of the container will dictate the size of the bottle, which can vary from a single serving juice bottle to a bleach bottle. You will want the water to leak out slowly, so do not make the hole too big. The hole may be in the cap, or the bottom of the container. If it is in the cap, cut off the bottom of the container and sink the neck of the bottle into the soil. Another method is to place cloth wicks in the pots when they are being planted. The wick trails out of the drainage hole in the bottom of the pot into a basin of water below the plant.

Probably one of the easier methods is to use a product called Terra Sorb, which is added to the potting mix. It is a crystal that turns into a gelatinous substance that absorbs many times its weight in water, acting as a water reservoir. Its main drawback is that it keeps the soil very wet during the rainy season and the plants may rot. The package suggests that holes can be made in the soil and the crystals added to plants that are already potted up. If you do this, add only a very small amount of the crystals; they expand when watered and will bubble up onto the soil surface, looking not unlike slug eggs.

Container gardens require fertilizing more often because the nutrients are leached out with the frequent watering. The fertilizer in the soil mix will last about six weeks if it was a granular fertilizer like 6-8-6 and two to three months if it was a slow-release type. Keep in mind that these are merely estimates, because the length of time the fertilizer lasts depends on the temperature and how often the container is being watered. Mix up a fertilizer solution like 20-20-20, 6-8-6 or fish fertilizer at half-strength, and water the plants with it once a week during the rest of the summer. Half-strength means that twice as much water is used when the fertilizer is mixed or half the amount of fertilizer is used with the full amount of water. You can use full-strength fertilizer every two weeks instead, but the results are better if the plants receive a more constant supply of nutrients.

Raised Beds

Raised beds are not unlike large containers. They have many applications in the garden and can be any size that is convenient and will fit into the layout of the garden. Raised beds bring the root zone above ground level, so the soil warms up faster in the spring and water drainage is improved. They give the vegetable garden a tidy appearance and the beds are easier to weed. The ease of weeding may be partly psychological—somehow confined areas are not as overwhelming as a great expanse of garden. The height of the raised bed can be anywhere from a few inches (centimetres) to several feet (metres) or more, and will be dictated by its intended use. If the height of the bed is such that the gardener can sit on the edge of the bed or garden from a chair, it is easier on the back. The bed should be just wide enough that you can comfortably reach to the center if it is a freestanding bed or to the back of the bed if it is accessible only on one side.

Raised beds can be made out of any building material, but some will last better than others. Those made out of plywood tend to rot after five years or so. Railroad ties are sturdy, but they should not have fresh creosote oozing out of them; use old ties that are well weathered. If the creosote is a concern, the beds can be lined with .1 mm (4-mil) polyethylene film (plastic) and place a lining of untreated plywood over the plastic. Copper napthanate is painted on treated timber. It is safe to use in the vegetable garden as long as it has dried before the soil is added. Never use wood that has been treated with chlorophenol (PCP) products for any garden projects. Brick, stone and cinder blocks can be used to build raised beds and the stone or brick will look very elegant.

Raised beds use a lot of soil. If they are being built in an existing garden, remove the topsoil, including the soil in the pathways, to add to the raised bed once it is built. The soil in the bottom of the bed may be of a poorer quality than the top 12 to 18 inches (30 to 45 cm) of soil.

The distance between the beds should be wide enough to move easily and you should be able to get a wheel barrow between them.

It is a good idea to plan the area on paper first, because once a bed is built it is not easy to move! Don't be afraid to be adventuresome—the beds can be laid out in a pleasing design. The food garden at UBC is an example of a very attractive raised-bed garden.

Once the beds are filled, the soil should not be walked on even if the raised bed is only a few inches off the ground. The only exception is in the fall when the soil is dug. The soil should be replenished with compost and manure yearly. Spread a layer over the soil and dig it under when the garden is dug in the fall. Like any other garden, the crops should be rotated each season.

Keen gardeners can get a head start on the season by using cold frames, hot beds and other covers. But extending the season does not just mean getting the seeds in earlier in the spring. In warmer areas of the province the gardening season can last much longer than the summer months. The fall rains do not have to mean that the garden is finished. Like the rest of the garden, however, it must be planned in advance. Plants that will overwinter, such as spinach and cabbage, must be sown in the summer, because plants do not grow much once the temperature drops and the level of light is low. By using cold frames and growing hardy vegetables late into the fall and winter, many gardeners can enjoy fresh vegetables from their garden most of the year. Unfortunately, winter gardening is not possible in all areas of the province, but experiment with extending the season in your garden.

Cold Frames

Cold frames are wonderful: they extend the range of plants that can be grown during the winter and give you a head start in the spring. No garden should be without one. Ideally they are placed against a protected, south-facing wall on a well-drained site. A cold frame can be purchased prebuilt, or it can be built with scrap lumber and an old window for the lid. Purchased ones usually have glass sides as well as a lid, which provides better light, but they are not as well insulated as those with wooden sides. The lid is hinged so it can be raised or lowered, allowing easy access to the plants and ventilation.

There are no hard and fast rules about how a cold frame should be built. The sides can be made out of stone or cinder blocks. The top can be glass, clear plastic—either rigid or soft, fiberglass, or any other type of transparent material. They can be any length but cannot be too wide; you must be able to reach to the back of the frame. An average size is 3 by 6 feet (1 by 2 m).

The back of the cold frame is about 18 inches (45 cm) in height and the sides slope to a front that is 8 inches (20 cm) in height. You can use copper naphthanate as a wood preservative, but allow it to dry before the soil is added to the frame. Do not use creosote as a preservative.

Cold frames are used to overwinter plants, start seedlings, force bulbs, protect plants during the winter and to harden off plants in the spring. For added insulation, for winter use, the top of the cold frame can be insulated with plastic and earth can be piled up around the frame.

The frame can also be heated with a light bulb or a string of Christmas lights if the temperature drops too low.

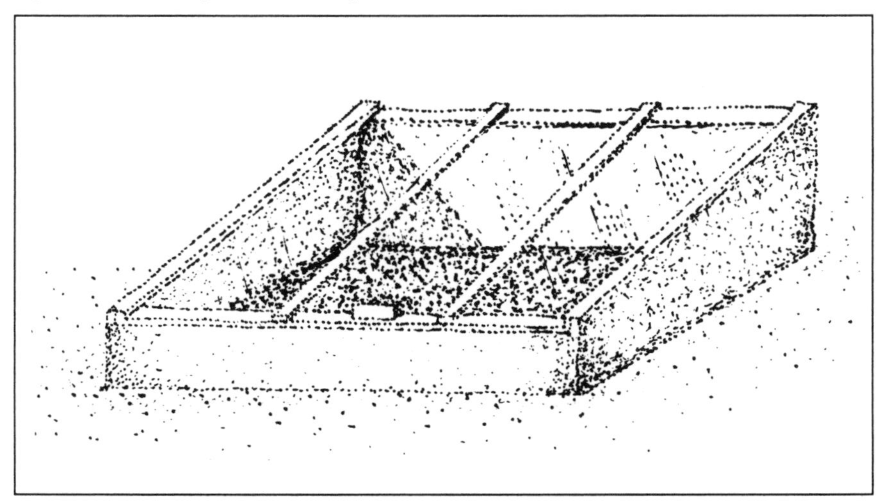

Cold frames are invaluable for protecting tender plants.

Hot Beds

Hot beds are simply cold frames with some type of heating. They are a luxury; they let you get plants out earlier in the spring and are a big help when propagating by protecting the cuttings and providing a good rooting environment.

Traditionally the beds were built over fresh manure, which produces heat as it decomposes. Today electric heating cables are used to provide bottom heat. To make a hot bed, construct a frame and place a layer of drainage material—either sand or stones—in the bottom of the bed. The heating coil is laid zigzag fashion back and forth along the length of the bed. Cover the coil with soil. A thermostat bulb attached to the heating coil is placed in the soil that covers the unit.

Take care when working in a bed with cables not to damage them by using tools carelessly. Some people place a wire mesh over the coils to protect them from damage.

Raised Beds

Raised beds, discussed also in Chapter 4, are another way to sow earlier in the spring. They warm up faster than the soil in the ground and the excess water drains more quickly. Raised beds can be made from wood 4 x 4s, stone, or other such material.

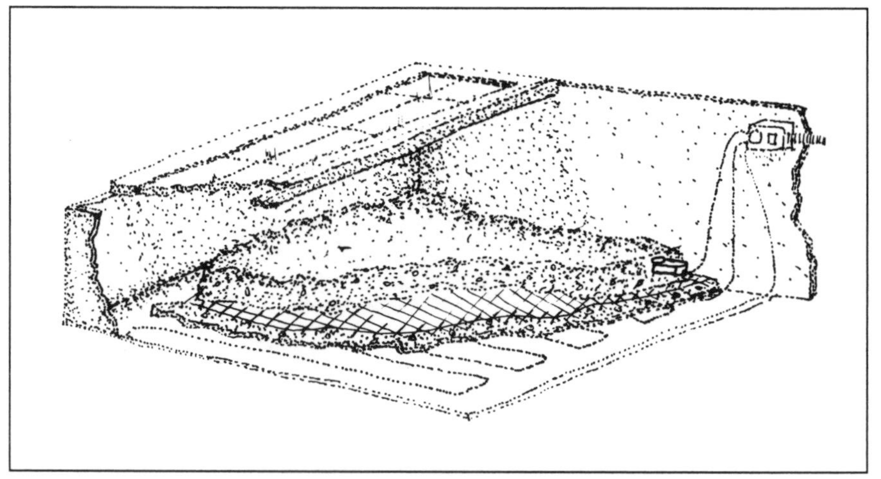

Heating cables warm the soil, which improves the germination rate.

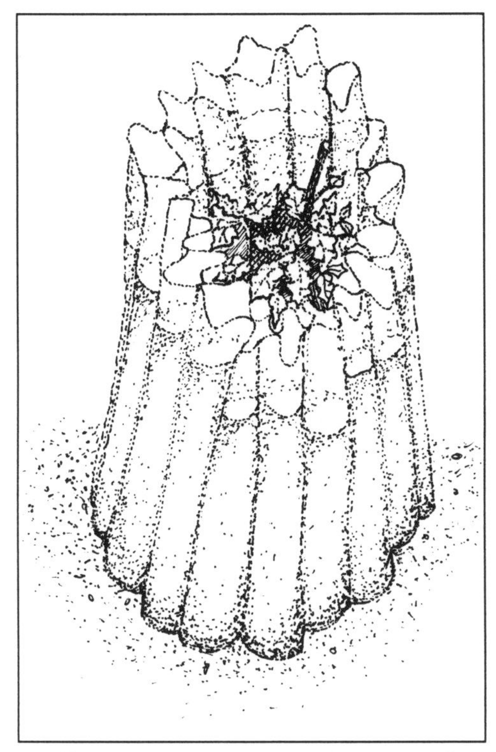

Wall-O-Water traps the sun's rays and warms the air around the plant.

A raised bed does not have to be a structure; it can be made by mounding the soil or digging trenches between the beds. Mounding the soil is often used for squash, pumpkins or cucumbers. It is very straightforward: just heap up the soil to about a foot (30 cm). Soil that is higher than the path between the beds will warm up faster in the spring. Dig the trench about 6 inches (15 cm) deep along the length of each side of the bed. The bed should be flat on top; if the beds are in the same spot each year it cuts down on soil compaction, because you will walk in the same path all the time. Instead of digging a trench, you can use the soil from the path to fill to the bed, so that you are lowering the path while raising the bed. Raised beds are not only good for getting a jump on the season, but can be used for growing winter vegetables.

Soil should be light, loamy and drain quickly so that it does not stay too wet. Clay soils hold the water and they are not suitable for early planting. Soil that contains a lot of organic matter will also stay cold longer; it holds water and is slower to heat up than soil that contains more air. Conversely, soil with organic material cools down more slowly in the fall. The organic matter acts as a buffer so the soil temperature will not have great extremes in temperature. The soil should not be mulched early in the spring because it will slow down the warming process. Soil for winter planting must also drain well so that the roots will not become waterlogged.

Temporary Covers

There are many temporary ways to protect plants. Covering the plants with plastic or glass not only protects them, but helps to warm the soil. It is essential to have a cover that is easily raised to get at the plants, and light must be able to get through the cover. The plastic must be raised on sunny days or the plants will quite literally cook—the temperature can get quite high under a clear covering. The plastic may have slits in it to increase the ventilation and it must be securely fastened to withstand the wind.

To cover a permanent bed with plastic, cross two poles at each end of the bed and lay another pole lengthwise on top of the crossed poles. Then you can simply drape clear plastic over the pole. The side can be rolled up on sunny days and dropped down again at night. Anchor the plastic on the ground with boards or soil. Once the warm weather comes, the structure is easily removed.

Small plants can be covered with plastic milk jugs that have had the bottoms removed. Wall-O-Water is a commercial product consisting of a water-filled ring of tubes that absorbs heat in the day and radiates the heat at night to keep the plant warm. There are portable plastic cloches available that will fit over individual plants or cover whole rows like a long plastic tunnel. (Cloche is a term that is used for a variety of glass or plastic structures that will protect plants from the cold.) Cloches can be made at home, or they are available from nurseries or catalogues. They should not be air-tight, because plants need fresh air to help prevent disease.

To make a tunnel cloche at home, place wire hoops in the ground; they should be tall enough to cover the crop, approximately 12 to 18 inches (30 to 45 cm) from the ground to the top. Place the hoops about 2 feet (60 cm) apart and cover them with clear plastic. Gather the ends

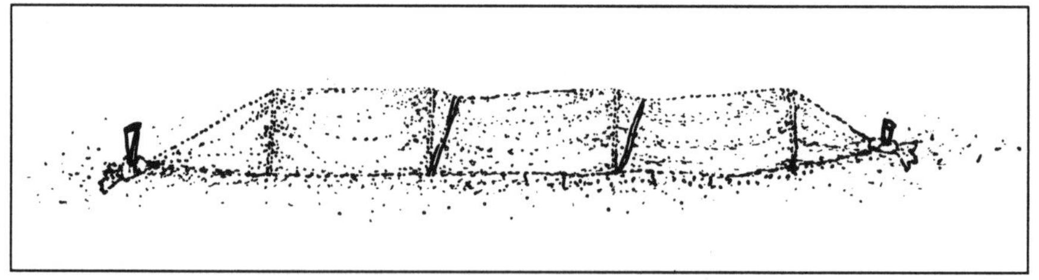

Row covers can protect whole rows or blocks of plants.

together and tie them around a stake in the ground. Clothespins can be used to hold the plastic to the hoops. On a hot day the plastic is rolled up on one side. The hoops can serve a dual purpose if they are left in the ground. In the summer they can be covered with Reemay or Agronet, a horticultural cloth that is used to protect a crop from insects and, to some extent, the weather.

You can also cover a tunnel with clear corrugated sheeting bent over hoops. A piece of plastic is placed at each end and held by a stake to enclose the tunnel.

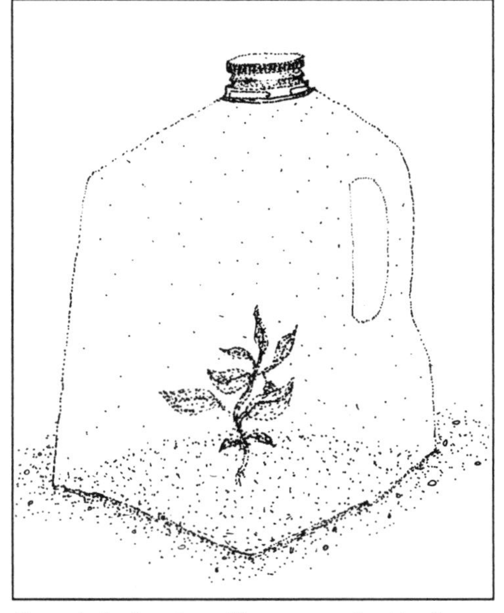

Recycled plastic milk jugs make ideal miniature greenhouses.

Plastic Mulch

Black plastic spread over the soil in the spring, two weeks before any tender crop is transplanted to the garden, will provide added warmth. The plastic is left on the soil through the growing season. Try it with melons, tomatoes and peppers.

To anchor the plastic, either nail it to the raised bed frames or place boards or soil over the edges. Using a garden fork, puncture the plastic at intervals. To plant, cut an X in the plastic for each transplant, and tuck the plants into the soil.

Black plastic will prevent weeds from growing. Clear plastic does a better job of raising the soil temperature, but weeds growing under it are a nuisance. Theoretically the sun will kill them, but it doesn't always happen. If you are gardening farther north where heat is most important, use clear plastic. Any plastic will also conserve moisture.

Floating Mulches

Floating mulches are fairly new on the gardening scene. They are clothlike materials that are placed over the crop when it is seeded or planted out. Sold under various trade names, such as Reemay or Agronet, they are made of spun bonded polyester. It is the same material used for interfacing garments, called Pellon. There are also other floating mulches on the market made out of polyethylene, polyester or polypropylene.

Floating mulches are used primarily as a way of keeping the crop insect free, but they also provide some weather protection. It keeps the temperature around the crop a few degrees warmer than the outer air, and cuts down on wind, although there may be some abrasion damage on the leaves. Crops that are overwintered under a floating mulch do better than those grown in the open. Those crops that require insect pollination, such as the squashes, must have the material removed when the plants begin to flower.

Floating mulches do not need to be supported by hoops, but are placed right on the crop or soil. Secure the sides of the cloth by pulling soil over the edges or using boards to hold it down. The cloth must be loose enough so the growing plants are not restricted. Crops such as carrots will benefit from lifting the cloth occasionally to help them push it up. When you lay the cloth down, make a lengthwise pleat down the middle to accommodate the extra cloth needed for the growing plants.

Greenhouses

Greenhouses will help to extend the vegetable season by giving a sheltered, heated place to grow vegetables during the winter. They can be used for starting transplants in the spring.

Winter Vegetables

The term winter vegetable is a bit of a misnomer because the vegetables do not do much growing. But they do remain green and, as they are leafy-type vegetables for the most part, such as spinach, chards and kale, they can be harvested leaf by leaf all during the winter. The plants must be sown, depending on the variety, from early summer through to the beginning of September. Depending on the area, some of the greens are sown in late August; the important thing to know is that they need enough growing time to size up before the cold weather stops their growth.

In areas where the soil doesn't freeze solid, you can leave some vegetables, such as carrots and parsnips, in the ground where they grew. It is a great place to store them. Brussels sprouts and leeks always taste better after a frost and continue to provide a harvest during the winter on the coast.

Overwintering Vegetable Varieties

CABBAGE Late cabbage is sown in the later part of June and early July for winter harvest; try 'January King', 'Winterstar' F1, and 'Savonarch' F1.

CAULIFLOWER 'Armando Spring Plus' (this package from Territorial Seeds contains seven different, winter-hardy, Walcherin types to extend the season), 'White Top' and 'Purple Cape' are all good varieties.

CORN SALAD This is a strong-flavored but very hardy plant that rather resembles a dandelion rosette. The leaves are tasty in a salad, especially when mixed with other greens. It is harvested either as a whole plant or leaf by leaf and it will put on additional growth in the early spring. The seeds can also be sown in the spring for summer harvest. It is usually marketed simply as corn salad.

ENDIVE Try sowing some in the cold frame for winter salads. It does not do well without protection because the water collects inside the loose head and causes rotting. Some varieties to try are 'Wivol', 'President', and 'Frisan'.

KALE Sow in the spring for winter harvest. Try growing 'Siberian', 'Green Curled Scotch' and 'Winter Red'.

LETTUCE Try using the cold frame to grow some lettuce. 'Winter Density' is a good choice.

SPINACH 'Tyee Hybrid' is a good winter producer.

Pest and disease control is essential to any garden. Nothing is more frustrating than to have the harvest ruined by insects or disease. In most cases, pests and diseases can be controlled by preventative measures, and by using environmentally safe cultural controls, and these are emphasized in this book. Vegetables that have been grown without using harmful chemicals are better for you as well as better for the environment.

The best way to have a disease- and pest-free garden is to raise healthy, stress-free plants.

- Give the plants adequate water and fertile soil.
- Do not overfertilize; lush green growth is very susceptible to insects and disease.
- Clean up garden trash and weeds. They are a perfect overwintering site for insects and disease. Sanitation is very important.
- Rotate your vegetable crops within the garden each year. Rotation is possible even in a tiny garden. Some insects and diseases only attack particular crops.

- Do not crowd the plants; allow room for air to circulate between the plants.
- Plant only healthy plants and use seed from reliable sources; some diseases are transmitted through the seed.
- Try not to injure the roots or the plants. The break in the tissue will leave an opening for insects and diseases to enter.
- Keep a daily watch for insects and remove them before their populations build up.
- Remember that not all insects are harmful! Some help to reduce other insect populations. Of course, like us, some insects are both helpful and destructive. Encourage ladybugs, lacewings, parasitic flies and wasps and spiders. Other insect predators, such as birds, bats, toads, frogs, and snakes, are welcome in the garden.
- If an area of the garden has a soil-borne disease, avoid moving soil or plants from that area to other parts of the garden.
- Dig the garden in the fall to expose insects, larvae and eggs to the cold and natural enemies—other insects and birds.
- Plant disease-resistant varieties.

However in some cases, despite all these efforts, a harvest may be lost and a chemical control may be the last resort. Any time a chemical is used on a food plant the label on the chemical container must be read carefully. Some chemicals are not registered for use on vegetables because they are harmful to humans. They may be systemic and absorbed into the plant rather than remaining on the surface. They may stay in the plant for too long; they may break down too slowly; or they may not be effective on the vegetable pests.

The number of days before harvest must always be observed. That is how long the chemical remains toxic on the plant after spraying. The date will vary from chemical to chemical and from crop to crop. Read the label for the information before the chemical is sprayed on any food crop.

Be wary of pesticides that are sold as organic, such as rotenone. Although it breaks down in one day, it is a very toxic chemical when it is being applied. Too often people think an organic-type spray is a safe chemical, but the same precautions apply to them as to other chemicals. There is controversy about rotenone, but I advise extreme caution regarding its use.

How to Use Chemicals

If you do decide to use chemicals, the following precautions may help to minimize the hazards.

- Use the correct chemical for the problem. An insecticide will not cure a fungus problem and vice versa.
- Read the directions each time the chemical is used. It is easy to forget, and when a new bottle is purchased the directions may have changed.
- Never increase or decrease the dosage. Too little may not be effective at all and too much may be equally or more ineffective. You could kill the plant and it can be harmful to you.
- Never mix different chemicals unless the directions say you can. The chemicals may not be compatible: you might make a lethal combination or they could nullify each other.
- Identify the insect or disease before you spray. It may not be necessary to use a chemical.
- Wear washable clothes, rubber gloves and a face mask when you spray. Wash your hands and face with soap after you have finished spraying. Do not spray chemicals if you have a health problem or are pregnant.
- Remove children and pets from the area; both of them have a great curiosity. All my cats have loved the fungicides and would get into treated seed packages or rub against plants I was spraying.
- Observe the number of days between spraying a chemical and harvesting; these are listed on the package.
- Always spray when the weather is calm; wait until dusk, when bees that can be harmed by the spray are in for the night.
- Do not contaminate water with pesticides, which are often lethal to fish. Do not let sprays drift or run off plants into the water.

- Never put chemicals into different containers or save unused portions. All chemicals should be kept under lock and key. Never use the same sprayer for herbicides and pesticides which include insecticides, miticides and fungicides. No matter how carefully the sprayer is cleaned there will be some herbicide residue left.
- Alternate chemicals so that pests and diseases do not build up a resistance to them.
- *If in doubt, don't!*

Pests and Diseases Common to Most Vegetables

Do not be discouraged by the long list of pests and diseases. Some will be a problem one year and will hardly be noticed the next, and others may never be a problem in your garden.

Pests that are specific to particular vegetables are dealt with in the encyclopedia section under the individual vegetable entries.

Pests

APHIDS are small, soft-bodied insects that are found on most vegetables, usually in large numbers. There are many species of aphids; they range in color from black and gray to yellow and pink, but they are most often green. Aphids can cause wilting and yellowing and may deform the plant growth. The aphid sucks the plant sap and may exude a sticky substance called honeydew, which can become moldy. Aphids can act as a vector, spreading viral diseases from one plant to another. There are usually several generations over the summer; most of them will be wingless. They overwinter on alternate hosts, which are often weeds.
Control: Remove the aphids as soon as they are spotted, before their population builds up. You can rub them off with your fingers or use water to squirt them off. If you are spraying young plants, be careful not to damage the tissues. A soap solution sprayed on the plant is effective. It must be repeated often and the whole plant must be covered. A mulch of aluminum foil placed on the ground seems to confuse aphids and they stay off the plants. Insecticidal soaps are effective on aphids.

CABBAGE LOOPERS are green caterpillars with a thin white stripe on both sides of their bodies. They are a common pest, particularly on kale crops, but they also leave holes in celery, beets, lettuce, peas, spinach and tomatoes. The adult is a gray moth that lays the eggs on the surface of leaves. Several generations will be born during the summer. The larvae feed for several weeks before they pupate.
Control: Hand-pick the larva and cover the crops with a floating mulch, such as Reemay or Agronet. A biological control, nontoxic to humans, is BT or *Bacillus thuringiensis*. A bacteria that is toxic only to caterpillars, it is sold as Thuricide or Dipel.

CABBAGE MAGGOTS are a serious pest of members of the Brassica family, attacking broccoli, Brussels sprouts, cabbage, cauliflower, turnip and rutabaga. The maggot tunnels into the root, killing or weakening the plant. The adult is a gray fly and there are two or three generations each summer. These maggots are difficult to control.
Control: Destroy all crop debris, control weeds and use a floating mulch like Reemay when the crop is seeded.

IMPORTED CABBAGEWORMS This is another caterpillar that attacks the kale crops, turnips and radish. It is the green larva of the pretty white butterfly that flits around the vegetable garden. It has three to five generations in a summer, and the larvae can do a lot of damage and leave unpleasant debris inside the plants. Use the same controls listed for cabbage loopers.

CUTWORMS There are two types of cutworms, those that feed below the soil surface, or wrap their body around the stem at ground level cutting the whole plant off, and those that climb into the plant to feed.
Subterranean Cutworms. There are two species, a red-backed cutworm and a dark-sided cutworm. The adults are brown or gray, nondescript, thick-bodied moths. The larvae attack most vegetables; they feed at night, causing the most damage in the late spring. There is only one generation each year and the eggs overwinter.
Control: Remove trash and weeds. The eggs (about 1,000 for each adult) are laid on the soil under plants and trash. The larva curls around the stem to feed, which can be prevented by a variety of home remedies. You can split drinking straws and place them over the stems, wrap the stem with tinfoil or cardboard, or place a twig on either side of the stem. If you

are using a straw, cardboard or tinfoil collar, place it 1 inch (2.5 cm) into the soil and have it extend about 2 inches (5 cm) up the stem. The collars are time-consuming but very effective. To help prevent overwintering, dig the garden in the fall to expose the eggs and remove trash and weeds.
Climbing cutworms. The bertha and black armyworms and the variegated cutworm are sporadic pests. They feed at night and will attack most vegetables, sometimes totally defoliating a plant. The adults are dull-colored, small moths. The larvae are dull blackish brown through gray but with a shiny head. They have one or two generations in the summer and will cause damage over the whole summer. They are a big problem in new gardens that were sod previously.
Control: Keep the garden free of trash and hand pick the larvae as you see them. Dig the garden in the fall.

EARWIGS are about 1/2 inch (1 cm) long with a curved pincers at their tail end. They are reddish brown in color and they feed at night, on all parts of most vegetables. They hide in plants like cabbage, lettuce and corn, and are a nuisance when the plants are harvested. There is one generation per year and it is the adults that overwinter. This insect is also a benefit, as it feeds on other insect larvae and aphids.
Control: They hide during the day, so cardboard tubes or rolled up paper make effective traps. Collect the traps often and burn them, or otherwise destroy them.

FLEA BEETLES make small holes in the leaves. The Colorado cabbage, hop and tuber flea beetles are the most common species. They attack many different crops and they are quite happy to move on to the next one. Vegetables that are on the preferrred eating list of flea beetles are beans, brassicas, peppers, potatoes and tomatoes. The larvae attack the roots. The adults are tiny black beetles that jump just as you are ready to get a good look at them. Unless the populations are high, they do not do too much damage. The exception is when plants are very small; then they have a problem recovering from the damage. There are one to two generations each year and the adults overwinter in the soil. Like many insect problems, some years they are worse than others and they are always worse in the late spring, especially if it is wet and cool.
Control: Clean up trash and dig the garden in the fall. Keep susceptible transplants inside until it is warm enough outside for them to grow quickly.

GRASSHOPPERS do little damage on the coast, but are more of a problem in the dryer areas, chewing the foliage on most vegetables. The main species are the clear-winged, red-legged, two-striped and migratory grasshoppers. There is usually one generation per year and they overwinter in the egg stage.
Control: Birds are a natural predator. Baits with Tangle Foot, molasses and bran attract grasshoppers and trap them in the sticky mess. The problem with this method is it also traps beneficial insects.

LEATHERJACKETS or **CRANE FLIES** are mainly a lawn pest, but will also attack most vegetables. They are a problem on the coast, where they feed on roots and foliage in the early spring. They are only a problem if their numbers are greater than 20 per square foot (30 cm squared). The larva of leatherjackets is leathery gray and maggotlike and it is found in the soil near the surface. To count the numbers, sink a bottomless can into the soil and pour a solution of soapy water into the can. The larvae will come to the surface where you can count them and estimate the number per square foot. The adult, which looks like a huge mosquito, is seen in late August or September. They have one generation and overwinter as larvae, which are vulnerable to the weather.
Control: Dig the soil in the fall and wait until April to do the larva count; many will perish over the winter.

NEMATODES are so tiny that you need a microscope to see them. They are parasites and will attack most vegetable crops, feeding mainly on root hairs or the surface cells. Some species do little damage and others do a lot. Some are vectors for viruses and others are beneficial and are used as biological controls for other insect pests. Those that feed a bit and move on do little damage, but others infest the plant, forcing it to produce special cells for the nematode to feed on. The root knot nematode (*Meloidogne)* and the potato cyst nematode (*Globodera*) will cause masses of tiny bumps or knots on the roots (do not confuse them with the nitrogen-fixing nodules on the legume crops).
Control: Rotate the crops and observe good garden sanitation; pull the whole plant up after harvesting the crop. Plant resistant varieties when they are available. I have heard that the gardeners at Sooke Harbour House on Vancouver Island use asparagus juice and seaweed as a natural nematocide.

SEEDCORN MAGGOTS can do a lot of damage during cool, wet springs, especially in soils with abundant organic matter. They will also attack beans, cucumber, onions, squash, peas, tomato and turnip. The fly has three or four generations per season. The maggot feeds on the seed and kills it, or causes the roots and shoots to be abnormal. In good growing years, when the weather is warm and dry, and for seeds sown later in summer, there will be no damage.
Control: To prevent seedcorn maggot damage, avoid seeding when the weather is damp and cold. Do not sow too deeply, as you want the seeds to germinate quickly. If a crop is damaged, dig the rows under and replant; it may not be reinfected by the maggot.

SLUGS are not an insect but a mollusc. They are pests in areas of high rainfall, where they enjoy the many shady, cool, damp hiding places. Slugs do not venture out in the heat of the day.

A slug can devour a whole plant at one sitting, and smaller slugs will hide in the leaves to dine over a number of nights. They leave a telltale trail of slime to mark their passage. The mass of white eggs are laid in the soil and all stages of the pest will overwinter. Slugs are active when the weather warms in the spring and this is the time to control them, before the vegetables are growing.
Control: Place boards between the rows for the slugs to hide under during the heat of the day. Turn them over daily and dispatch the slugs. Go out in the early morning or in the cool of the evening when the slugs are active. They are easy to see then and can be picked up easily and removed. Remove all trash that they can hide under; this includes bits of wood, weeds, old leaves and mulch. If the garden is overrun with slugs, do not use mulch until they are under control. Turn the garden in the fall, exposing the eggs for the birds and the winter frosts. Surround plants with a layer of crushed eggshells, ashes, coarse sand, or other gritty substances that will act as a barrier. If the garden is large and in the country, ducks will do an excellent job of eating slugs.

Slug bait, containing metaldehyde, can be set out early in the spring. Put the bait in a cottage cheese, yogurt or other disposable plastic container. Punch several holes near the bottom of the container, big enough for a slug to enter. The lid protects the bait from the rain, and animals and birds cannot get at the poisonous bait. Do not place bait where children might get at it. As an extra precaution, tape the lid shut with masking tape.

SNAILS The controls and information for slugs also apply to snails.

SPIDER MITES are tiny mites that can be seen only with a magnifying glass. They may be a problem under hot, dry conditions. The foliage will get a distinctive, speckled, brownish look and the leaves will curl, looking like they lack water. It is important to control spider mites at the first sign, as they reproduce often, having many generations each summer.
Control: Increasing the humidity around the plants discourages spider mites, which prefer dryer conditions. Insecticidal soap can be used to control mites.

THRIPS are tiny insects that are often missed by the home gardener because they can barely be seen by the naked eye. But the damage is characteristic, whether they are wrecking your gladiolus or attacking your onions. They also attack asparagus, beans, kale crops, cucumbers and tomatoes. They rasp off the outer layer of green cells, leaving a silvery look to the leaves. If you look closely at the damage it is often in parallel rows, made up of thousands of tiny dots. If there is extensive damage, the plants will be stunted and start to wilt, and the foliage will distort. Seen under a magnifying lens, thrips are yellow/brown and move quickly. There are several generations each summer. The numbers really build up when the weather is hot and dry, so most of the damage begins to show up in August and September.
Control: Destroy all garden refuse and weeds. Insecticidal soap can be used to control thrips.

WHITE GRUBS are the larvae of the ten-lined June beetle—the most common on the coast—and the June beetle. The larva is a large white grub with a brown head and a dark rear end. It attacks most vegetable roots, underground stems and tubers. The adults are seen flying in May and June. The insect takes three years to mature and both the adults and grubs overwinter. They may be a problem in a new garden that was previously a field.
Control: Dig the garden in the fall. Leave a new garden fallow the first year, keeping the weeds removed but not growing a crop. A new biological control called Biosafe kills the grubs with nematodes.

WIREWORMS are the larvae of the large, black or brown click beetle. There are many species and they live for several years in the soil,

attacking most vegetables. The larvae will damage seeds and underground stems of seedlings and transplants by tunneling into the roots, bulbs and tubers. The adults are garden scavengers and are good for the garden; unfortunately the larvae can be a problem.
Control: A piece of potato buried near susceptible crops will attract wireworms. Change the trap once a week, destroying the infested trap. Dig the garden in the fall.

PEA (BEAN) LEAF WEEVIL is a pest in the lower mainland of British Columbia and on Vancouver Island. The small brown weevil bites notches out of the leaves of both peas and beans. They have only one generation each year. The adult overwinters in the soil and becomes active in time to eat the seedlings that are just emerging. They often eat enough of the leaf that the seedling dies. It may look like the row of peas or beans has not germinated, or the row may have a lot of gaps.
Control: Rotate the crop each year and clean up all the debris after harvest. Pyrethrum, an organic control, can be used on a young crop. When the plants are mature they are able to withstand some damage without a loss in the yield.

Diseases

BACTERIAL BLIGHTS are the cause of several different diseases that show up as water-soaked spots on vegetables and large, brown, dead areas on the leaves. Some bacterial blights thrive in moist, warm weather and others do better in moist, cool weather. Some vegetables that are troubled with blight are beans, celery, kales, peas, peppers and tomatoes.
Control: Use disease-free seed, rotate the crop, and do not work around the plants when they are wet. The bacteria can get on clothing and then it is transferred to other plants along the row.

CLUBROOT causes yellowing and wilting of kale plants. Test for clubroot by uprooting one of the plants. If it has clubroot, the root will be enlarged, with wartlike growths. This disease is common to all the kale crops and is prevalent in acid coastal soils which favor the disease. Unfortunately it can persist in the soil for at least seven years.
Control: Increase the pH to above 7.2 to discourage the disease, and rotate the kale crops. Grow your own transplants to prevent accidental introduction of the disease into your garden. If you have the disease in

your garden, avoid growing kale crops for at least five, and preferably seven, years.

DAMPING-OFF is a soil-borne disease that rots seeds and attacks seedlings before they emerge or at the soil line. First the stem looks pinched just at soil level and then the seedling falls over and dies.
Control: Always use sterilized soil to start seeds indoors. When direct seeding in the garden, do not plant too early, when the soil is wet and cold. Sow seeds thinly so that there is air circulation between the plants. Cold frames should be opened when possible to allow air to circulate. Large seeds, such as peas and beans, are often treated with the fungicide thiram before they are purchased. If you prefer untreated seeds, many companies sell them either way.

DOWNY MILDEW is prevalent when the weather is cool and wet or when there are heavy dews. It shows up as white or purplish fuzzy patches on the vegetables and on their leaves. The symptoms will vary somewhat with the vegetable. It may also cause black or brown spots or streaks.
Control: Rotate the vegetables and remove all debris after harvest. Cultivate only when the plants are dry.

POWDERY MILDEW is a powdery, grayish white growth that shows up as summer progresses. It gradually spreads; in some cases it covers the entire leaf. When it infects young leaves, they may be distorted. It usually occurs late enough in the season that it is not a problem as far as yield is concerned. Plants that are always affected are the cucumber family, beans and peas.
Control: Destroy all infected foliage after the crop has been harvested. Select resistant varieties where possible, such as 'Comet 11' and 'Bush Baby' cucumbers.

GRAY MOLD is a soil-borne disease that usually starts where the vegetable touches the ground. Beans are particularly susceptible. Gray mold must have old dying tissue to live on before it can infect the pods; it often gets a start on the old blossom that adheres to the bean pod. The affected part becomes covered with a white or gray mold. If you look at it carefully, you will see hard, tiny, black seedlike structures, called sclerotia. They fall to the soil, to reinfect the next crop.

Control: Rotate the crop, and leave a space between plants so they are not touching each other. This will stop the disease from spreading from one plant to another. Clean up debris after the crop is harvested.

Weeds Are Pests Too

Weeds are plants that are survivors and they will out-compete most vegetables for water and nutrients, especially when the plants are young. The expensive fertilizer you use on the vegetable garden is wasted if it grows bigger and healthier weeds.

In every garden there are thousands of weed seeds just waiting to get close enough to the surface to germinate. The good news is the longer the garden is kept weed-free, the easier the weeding job becomes. The secret is to hoe the weeds when they are tiny, before they have a chance to set seed. When they are tiny they wither and die on the surface of the soil as they are hoed.

It is important to control perennial weeds before they become established. They have large root systems and many will spread with underground rhizomes.

The most important time to control weeds is in the spring when the vegetables are becoming established. Early weeds competing with the crop can reduce the yield by as much as 80 percent. Later in the season, weeds do not do as much damage but they will still harbor insects and are a source of disease.

Problems

Not all holes, spots and rots are caused by disease or insects—at least initially. Some problems, such as catfacing, blossom end rot and leaf curl in tomatoes, are mentioned in the encyclopedia section under the individual vegetable entries. None of these is caused by a pest or a disease, yet they look like they might be.

Herbicide damage can cause the leaves, stems and fruits to be deformed or have odd markings on them. Lawn formulas that contain a fertilizer and herbicide can drift from a distance if there is a wind, blowing from a neighboring lawn or from roadside spraying. Some vegetables, such as tomatoes, are very susceptible to herbicide damage and others may not show any damage. If there is any suspicion that plants have been contaminated by chemicals such as these, I strongly advise against eating them; it is not worth the risk.

Stunting of plants can be caused by cold weather or nutrient deficiencies. Fertilizer dropped onto wet leaves can cause spots on the leaves where it has burned the tissue. If the leaves are yellow and the plants are stunted it may be from lack of nutrients, soil compaction or wet soil—as well as insect and disease damage. Insect damage may sometimes cause a lack of fruit, but so can temperature extremes and too much nitrogen, among other factors.

7 Herbs

Herbs are generally herbaceous plants, grown as annuals, biennials or perennials, that are used to add flavor to our food. But through usage the term herb also includes some woody subshrubs, such as thyme and sage, which are not true perennials, and the odd tree such as the bay laurel (*Laurus nobilis*). Herbs not only flavor food but they have medicinal properties, and many are aromatic.

Herbs will grow in well-prepared garden soil, and some will even tolerate poorer soils. Many are very attractive and can be an asset to the garden. They can be planted in beds that are strictly for herbs; annual herbs can be grown in the vegetable garden; and any herb can be grown in with flowers, although some are more suitable than others. Smaller herbs are suitable for containers.

The earliest herbal was written on clay tablets around 3000 B.C. by Sumerians, who valued herbs for their magical and medicinal properties and scent. The fact that they flavored food was likely secondary to their other purposes. In the time of Imhotep (2700 B.C.) there was a pharmacopoeia containing 500 herbs and herbal recipes. Greek and Syrian women grew pots of herbs on the flat-topped roofs of their houses. Later the herbs and their uses were jealously guarded by the early priests.

During the Dark Ages, when towns became fortified, there was very little room for plants. The precious herbs were grown in small, raised, regimented beds. Small annual herbs were grown as clipped hedges between the beds.

Later, many herbs were grown in walled or hedged Physic Gardens that were the forerunners of today's botanical gardens. Even today we often grow herbs in formal plantings, although many look lovely growing in the flower garden.

In England, by 1200 B.C. many herbs, such as sage, hyssop, rue, camomile, betony and dill, were grown both in the kitchen garden for flavorings and the herb garden for medicine. Sage, which was brought to England by the Romans, was used to cleanse the body of venom and pestilence and as a flavoring for meats. A medieval proverb says "he that would live for aye must eat sage in May." Angelica, used as an antipestilant, was enjoyed for its aromatic oils in the roots, its seeds that flavored drinks (an ingredient in Chartreuse) and the stalks which were candied. Last but not least, angelica cured flatulence.

Annual Herbs	Biennial Herbs	Perennial Herbs
Anise	Parsley	Bee Balm
Basil		Catnip
Borage		Chives
Dill		Fennel
Sweet marjoram		Garlic
		Lovage
		Mint
		Sage
		Oregano
		Thyme
		Winter Savory

Encyclopedia of Common Herbs

ANISE *Pimpinella anisum*

Aniseed has a licorice flavor and smell. Its small white flowers are born in an umbel, like carrots and parsnips.

Height: 20 to 24 inches (50 to 60 cm).

Light and Soil: Full sun and fertile soil.

How to Grow: Sow the seeds directly outdoors as early as possible in the spring. Thin the plants to 6 inches (15 cm) apart.
Harvesting: As soon as the seeds start to turn dark, remove the seed head and dry it in a paper bag to catch the seeds.
Uses: The seeds are used to flavor desserts.
Problems: The plants will bolt in hot weather.

BASIL *Ocimum basilicum*

Sweet or common basil comes in many forms, scents and colors. The colors vary from a deep purple through various shades of green. There are lemon, cinnamon, anise and regular scented basils. It is truly a lovely addition anywhere in the garden.
Height: 8 to 24 inches (18 to 60 cm).
Light and Soil: Sun to light shade and fertile soil.
How to Grow: Add some compost to the soil to increase its moisture-holding capacity. Sow the seeds indoors and set out transplants or direct seed when the weather warms. Set the plants 8 to 10 inches (20 to 25 cm) apart.
Harvesting: Pick individual leaves as they are needed and freeze the excess.
Uses: The leaves are used to flavor pasta, meat, fish, cheese and tomatoes. The scented ones are used to flavor teas and fruit.
Problems: Pinch the plants back or they will become leggy.

BEE BALM *Monarda didyma*

Bee balm, or bergamot, is a North American native that is used to make Oswego tea. The flowers are an attractive red, although there are cultivars that are lavender through pink to white. The flowers attract hummingbirds and bees. The flowers remain attractive on into the fall and the plant is frequently sold as an ornamental.
Height: 3 feet (90 cm).
Light and Soil: Sun to partial shade and a good garden soil.
How to Grow: It is grown from seed, divisions and cuttings.
Harvesting: The leaves and flowers are harvested during the summer and used fresh or dried.
Uses: Bee Balm is used to flavor tea and fruit dishes and to make potpourri.
Problems: It can escape the garden to become a weed.

BORAGE *Borago officinalis*

Borage is a tall plant with hairy leaves. Its only saving grace as a decorative plant is its incredible blue flowers.

Height: 3 feet (90 cm).

Light and Soil: Plant in the full sun and it will tolerate poor soil.

How to Grow: Borage is either started as transplants or direct-seeded in the spring. Do not cover the seed as it needs light to germinate. The plants can be pruned to keep them lower but the flowers will be sacrificed.

Harvesting: Harvest tender leaf tips and flowers.

Uses: The flowers are edible and used to decorate salads and deserts. They may be candied. The fresh leaves are used in salads.

CATNIP *Nepeta cataria*

Catnip is not a very attractive plant once it is full grown, but its soft, furry leaves certainly attract my cat.

Height: 3 feet plus (over 90 cm).

Light and Soil: Sun or partial shade and good garden soil enriched with compost to hold moisture.

How to Grow: Seeds are started indoors and transplants set out once the weather warms. If you have a cat, protect the seedlings until the plant becomes established.

Harvesting: Harvest the tender new leaves and flowers and dry them.

Uses: Catnip is used for tea and for the cat to roll in.

Problems: It does spread and can become weedy.

CHIVES *Allium schoenoprasum*

Chives are one of the most attractive herbs. Their round purple flower clusters attract bees.

Height: 8 to 12 inches (20 to 30 cm).

Light and Soil: Grow them in the sun in rich, moist soil.

How to Grow: Chives grow easily from seed, either direct-seeded, as transplants or from division. They are not weedy; although they freely seed themselves, the seeds are heavy, dropping to the ground to germinate rather than blowing around. The excess plants are left to grow, transplanted or weeded out to go into the salad. To keep the young growth coming, cut back half the plant to 2 inches (5 cm). After it has sent up new shoots, cut back the rest of the plant.

When to Harvest: The onionlike leaves may be harvested anytime and

frozen to preserve them.
Uses: Cut up the leaves for soup and salads. The young flower heads are used in salads.

DILL *Anethum graveolens*

Dill weed has earned its name because it has naturalized in the landscape. It sets its seed just in time to be added to jars of homemade dill pickles.
Height: 3 to 5 feet (90 to 150 cm).
Light and Soil: Plant in full sun in most garden soils.
How to Grow: Sow the seeds directly in the garden in the spring.
Harvesting: All parts of the plant may be used. If the seeds are to be harvested, pick the whole head just as the seeds turn brown. Put the head in a paper bag to catch the seeds as they ripen.
Uses: The plant may be used fresh in salads, soups, stews and dill pickles.
Problems: It can become invasive.

FENNEL *Foeniculum vulgare*

Fennel is a half-hardy perennial on the coast, but it is treated as an annual in colder areas. It has very attractive feathery bronze or green foliage early in the spring, but it fast becomes a very tall plant that will overwhelm a small garden. It can be pruned, but then it will not flower. When children smell the crushed leaves or seeds, they say it smells like black jelly beans.
Height: 4 to 6 feet plus (over 1.2 to 1.8 m).
Light and Soil: Full sun in rich garden soil.
How to Grow: Direct seed the plants in the spring. On the coast, seedlings will pop up all over the garden, but unwanted ones are easy to pull out.
When to Harvest: All parts of the stem, leaves or seeds may be harvested. When the seeds are ripe, they are easy to shake into a bag.
Uses: Use the leaves fresh in salads or wrap them around cooking fish.
Problems: Only its size.

GARLIC *Allium sativum*

Garlic is a perennial bulb that dies back to the ground each year, but, of course, the bulbs are harvested. This is a herb that is sometimes baked whole and served as a vegetable.

Height: 2 feet (60 cm).
Light and Soil: Full sun in compost-enriched soil.
How to Grow: On the coast, plant the bulb divisions 4 inches (10 cm) apart in late fall. In colder areas, plant the cloves in early spring.
Harvesting: On the coast, garlic will be ready to harvest at the beginning of August and in colder areas about three months after planting. Hang to dry in a shady, frost-free place.
Uses: Flavoring meat dishes, soups and salads.

LOVAGE *Levisticum officinale*

Lovage is a tall perennial plant that will need sturdy staking later in the summer. Like fennel, it needs to be planted at the back of the garden. It has a strong, celerylike taste and when the leaves are rubbed it smells like celery.
Height: 4 to 6 feet plus (1.2 to 1.8 m).
Light and Soil: Plant lovage in full sun in rich soil that has been amended with compost to hold moisture.
How to Grow: Start the plants from seed, divide the plant, or purchase a transplant. Lovage is slow to grow from seed. One plant is adequate for a home garden. Lovage needs to be well watered. Like most perennials, the plant will need to be divided every five years or so.
Harvesting: Harvest the leaves and stems throughout the summer. The seeds are easily shaken into a bag after they ripen and darken in the fall.
Uses: Lovage can be used fresh in salads, soups and stews. The seeds are used to flavor meats and breads.

MARJORAM *Origanum marjorana*

Sweet marjoram is a pretty, low-growing annual that is related to oregano. Marjoram is a half-hardy perennial that is usually grown as an annual.
Height: 12 to 24 inches (30 to 60 cm).
Light and Soil: Grow in full sun in good garden soil that has been amended with lime if the soil is acidic.
How to Grow: Sweet marjoram tends to be slow from seed; purchased plants or divisions are best.
Harvesting: Use the tender top leaves and stems. Harvest it just as the flower buds begin to develop. Use it fresh or dry the leaves.
Uses: Sweet marjoram is used in soups, meat dishes, stuffings and in potpourri.

MINT *Mentha* spp.

There are several different mints—peppermint, spearmint, lemon mint and apple mint—all with different flavors and scents. Mints are hardy perennials and some of the mint cultivars are more attractive than others.
Height: 1 to 3 feet (30 to 90 cm).
Light and Soil: Mints will tolerate a range of conditions, from full sun to shade. They need moist, rich soil.
How to Grow: Not all mints breed true from seed, so they are usually started from runners (a stem that grows horizontally and has a new plant at the tip) or root division. Plant mints in containers or separate beds, as the runners spread through the garden. Cut back several times during summer to force new growth. Fertilize the plants after pruning.
Harvesting: Harvest the tender new leaves throughout the summer. The leaves can be dried.
Uses: Mint is used to flavor lamb and candy and to make tea and potpourri.
Problems: Mint is very invasive.

OREGANO *Origanum* spp.

Oregano is usually sold in the store as a package of mixed herbs—different species of oregano, sage and thyme—rather than a particular plant. Oregano is a perennial and the different species have a range of hardiness.
Height: 6 to 10 inches (15 to 25 cm).
Light and Soil: Plant oregano in full sun and add lime to the soil if it is acidic. It will tolerate poor soil.
How to Grow: Start plants from seed, cuttings or division. They can be pruned back when they start to flower to encourage new growth.
When to Harvest: Harvest the new leaves throughout the summer. The leaves will dry very quickly.
Uses: Try oregano in soups, tomato dishes and stews. Whole stems with flowers can be dried to use in floral arrangements.

PARSLEY *Petroselinum crispum*

Parsley is best known as that curly bit of green on the side of the plate, although it has a wide range of culinary uses. There are several very attractive forms of parsley, some with a curlier leaf than other. It is biennial or sometimes a short-lived perennial. It is a good candidate for containers, and it is not out of place in the flower border.

Height: 6 inches (15 cm).
Light and Soil: Plant in full sun or light shade in good garden soil that has had compost added.
How to Grow: Start seeds inside in the spring. It comes very readily from seed and it will seed freely in the garden.
Harvesting: The fresh leaves can be harvested as soon as the plant is established. The whole plant can be pruned back and it will send out new growth. Use the leaves fresh, or they may be frozen or dried. Parsley will keep fresh in water for several days or a week in a plastic bag in the refrigerator.
Uses: Use parsley as a garnish and in soups, stews and stuffings.
Problems: They sometimes get aphids which can be sprayed off with water or treated with insecticidal soap.

SAGE *Salvia officinalis*

There are several attractive varieties of sage that are an asset to the garden. The common sage has gray green leaves; there are also golden, purple and tricolor forms.
Height: 1 to 2 feet (30 to 60 cm).
Light and Soil: Grow sage in full sun and add some lime to the soil if it is acidic.
How to Grow: Sage grows readily from seed sown indoors in the spring and from cuttings or division.
Harvesting: Harvest the tender leaves and shoots. The leaves dry easily. Branches can be dried to use in flower arrangements.
Uses: Sage is blended with other herbs to use in poultry stuffing and in Italian herb mixtures. Use in stews, meat and tomato dishes.

SAVORY *Satureja montana*

Winter savory is a strong-flavored, attractive perennial.
Height: 8 to 12 inches (20 to 30 cm).
Light and Soil: Plant in full sun in soil that has been ammended with lime if it is acidic.
How to Grow: Savory grows readily from seed started indoors 8 weeks before they are planted out.
Harvesting: Harvest the tender leaves. It can be harvested lightly during the winter.
Uses: Savory is used fresh or dry in stews, meats, legume dishes and stuffings.

THYME *Thymus vulgaris*

Thyme is a very attractive, low-growing, woody herb that is sometimes used as a ground cover or between stones on a path. It has purple flowers, and some cultivars have a more intense color than others.

Height: 4 to 6 inches (10 to 15 cm).

Light and Soil: Thyme does best in full sun but it will tolerate some shade. Plant it in good garden soil augmented with compost.

How to Grow: Thyme may be grown from seed, cuttings or division. Divide the plant every five years or when the middle growth is sparse.

Harvesting: Harvest the tips of the branches and use them fresh or dried. Whole branches may be dried and tied in bundles for their fragrance.

Uses: Thyme is used in meat dishes, soups and stews.

The vegetables in the following encyclopedia are those commonly grown in British Columbia. Harvesting, optimum growing conditions and growing instructions have been included in each entry.

Common insect pests and diseases are listed for each entry. Information on those pests and diseases common to many vegetables can be found in chapter six, Pests and Diseases. If they are restricted to a particular vegetable, they are discussed with that entry only.

Varieties that do well in the coastal region, including some of the latest varieties and many older ones that are worth growing, have been noted. New varieties are introduced each year; do not hesitate to try them to see how they will do in your garden.

ASPARAGUS *Asparagus officinalis*

Asparagus is a very hardy perennial crop that will continue to produce for twenty years or more. The young spears appear early in the spring, rivaling rhubarb as one of the earliest crops to be harvested.

Asparagus is one of the plants that the Greeks and Romans grew in their gardens. It's hard to believe that it belongs to the same family as lilies, but there is some resemblance. Asparagus is also related to asparagus fern, a house plant. It has escaped the garden and grows wild in many parts of B.C., spread by the birds that eat the berries in the late summer.

There are both male and female asparagus plants. The female has red berries and produces thick spears. The male is more prolific and the spears are thinner. Unlike some plants, such as kiwi, it is not necessary to have both male and female plants to produce the spears. The plants grow easily from seed, but it takes three to four years before they produce a harvestable crop. Usually two-year-old crowns with roots are purchased in the spring. The crowns are the growing point of the plant, where the leaves will emerge when it starts to grow.

Asparagus requires a lot of room and a permanent site. After the crop is harvested, the plants produce tall, attractive, fernlike foliage which can be used in floral arrangements. Asparagus can be planted in the back of a flower border rather than in the vegetable garden. It is already harvested by the time the perennials are up or the annuals planted.

Harvest Time: Spring.

Height: At 5 to 7 inches (13 to 18 cm) the spears are ready to be harvested. The foliage grows up to 4 to 6 feet (1 to 2 m) and an older clump can attain a spread of about 6 feet (2 m).

Light and Soil: Asparagus will tolerate light shade. The plants require a permanent bed with well-drained, fertile soil. Work well-rotted manure or other organic matter into the soil. It is important to prepare the soil well because the bed will be undisturbed for many years. If the drainage is poor, mound the soil to form a raised bed. Asparagus responds very well if the soil is mulched with seaweed. The old English garden books suggest top-dressing the soil with salt once a year. It is suspected the salt may help to reduce root rots, and 3 ounces (85 gm) of rock salt per square yard (metre) of soil may be used once a year in the early spring.

How to Grow: Dig a trench 10 inches (25 cm) deep, mounding the soil the length of the trench down the center. Spread the roots over the mound, spacing them 12 to 18 inches (30 to 50 cm) apart within the row. The crown should be about 8 inches (20 cm) deep and it must be covered with 2 inches (5 cm) of soil. Gradually add more soil as the plants grow over the summer.

Asparagus is a heavy feeder and the beds will require mulching in the spring with rotted manure. Broadcast a balanced fertilizer like 6-8-6 in July. It is important that the plants get adequate water, especially in the first year, to encourage the plants to grow deep roots. Weed control is a must because the young plants cannot compete with the weeds for food and water. It is particularly important for a perennial crop because it will produce for many years if it is well established in the early years.

Remove the fronds in the fall, especially if the plants have had any insect or disease problems during the growing season. In colder areas, if the fronds were healthy, leave them on the plants until spring cleanup. The old fronds will trap snow, which will give the roots some insulation from the cold.

Harvesting: Do not harvest the spears the first two years after transplanting. In succeeding years, gradually increase the number of weeks the plant is harvested, starting with two weeks and building up to eight weeks. Pick spears with tight heads and cut them with a sharp knife 1 inch (2.5 cm) below ground level. In established beds the spears are harvested daily until the new spears become thin and spindly.

Storage: Asparagus is usually eaten fresh and is at its peak eaten immediately after harvesting. It can be refrigerated in a plastic bag for several days before cooking. Asparagus can be frozen and used later in soups or other cooked dishes.

Pests and Diseases: Asparagus is susceptible to damage from cutworms and aphids. For more information about these problems, see chapter six, Pests and Diseases.

Asparagus beetle attacks asparagus in both the adult and larval stage, causing damage to the developing spears. The adult is a small, blue black, fast-moving beetle with three large cream-colored (yellow orange) spots. The black eggs are noticeable, as they are attached singly in a row on the fronds. There are two to three generations over the summer.

The adults can be picked off the plants and the foliage that has the eggs attached to it should be destroyed. Destroy all foliage in the fall if you have had any insects over the summer. Lady beetle (alias ladybug, although it's really a beetle) larvae will eat the eggs and larvae of the asparagus beetle. Pyrethrum should only be sprayed if a large number of beetles have been observed. Killing the adults as soon as they appear prevents them from laying their eggs and this will reduce the numbers of succeeding generations. Read the directions on the container before using any pesticide.

Twelve-spotted asparagus beetle is an occasional pest that does little damage as it feeds only on the foliage and berries of the asparagus plant. Use the same controls for the twelve-spotted beetle as for the asparagus beetle.

Asparagus aphid damage includes stunting of plants, death of seedlings, and reduction of yield and vigor in established plants. The insect is waxy and powdery green in color. It is found only in the southern interior of British Columbia. To help prevent infestation, remove the old fronds in the fall or early in the spring.

Rust produces elongated, reddish brown spots on the spears and fronds. To prevent rust, destroy the fronds in the fall and plant resistant varieties. During the growing season water early in the day if a sprinkler is used, to allow the foliage time to dry before night falls.

Varieties: 'Mary Washington', 'California 500' and 'Viking' are rust-resistant varieties. 'Martha Washington' is a well-known variety that has been grown for many years; it is fairly rust resistant. When plants are purchased there is often little choice, because garden centers usually carry only one variety. If you want a particular variety, phone around and check the catalogues. Many carry the plants as well as seed.

Hint: If you want a very productive asparagus bed, keep only the male plants and pull out the plants that bear berries.

BEANS ***Phaseolus vulgaris*** **and** ***P. coccineus***

There are many varieties of bean; all of them are warm-weather crops with the exception of broad beans. All beans grown in B.C. are annuals. Bush beans (*Phaseolus vulgaris*) produce their crop all at once over a short period of time and may be sown successively until the first week in July. Pole beans (*P. vulgaris*) and runner beans (*P. coccineus*) are sown in the spring; they continue to produce over a longer period of time and may be picked right through until fall. Broad beans (*Vicia faba*) are treated differently because they are hardier, and are covered in a separate entry.

Beans are an ancient crop that were known to the Greeks and Romans, while other varieties were grown in the New World. Lima beans are named for the capital city of Peru, and beans have been found inside ancient tombs in South America.

String bean was a common name that was in use until about fifty years ago, when breeders developed varieties without the tough string that ran along the seam of the pod. The new bean that was developed was known as a snap bean because it was now easy to break or snap a fresh bean in half.

Legume roots form nodules that contain bacteria, rhizobia, which convert nitrogen in the air into a form the plant can use. If the beans are given a high-nitrogen fertilizer, the plants will become leggy, the yield will drop and few nodules will be formed. Why the nodules don't form is not fully understood, but it appears the need for nitrogen must be there before the legume and the rhizobia can interact. Feed the plants a fertilizer like 6-8-6 that is low in nitrogen but higher in phosphorus. The seedlings need some nitrogen until the bacteria becomes established on its roots.

Bacteria inoculants which contain rhizobia can be purchased to increase what is naturally in the soil. This is helpful in new gardens that have not had a previous legume crop. There are many different species of rhizobia, so buy the bacteria strain suitable for the crop you are growing. The package will state what crops it is suitable for inoculating. Some inoculants can be used for several different crops, including beans, peas and sweet peas; others are plant-specific. Refrigerate the inoculant until you use it, and buy it from a reliable dealer to insure that it is fresh. If you want to learn more about inoculants, consult *Soil Science Simplified*, by Harpstead, Hole and Bennett, listed in the bibliography at the back of this book.

Bush beans include snap, wax, bush, purple or green beans. They are low-growing plants that produce their whole crop over a very short period of time. To extend the crop, plant successive sowings every two weeks from May until the first week of July.

Pole beans are snap, wax or green beans that grow 6 to 7 feet (1.8 to 2 m) in height. The plants will need support. You can use netting or chicken wire supported on poles to make a trellis. The support should be sturdy, as the full-grown plants will be heavy. A teepee can be easily made for pole beans to climb on. Tie the ends of three 7-foot (2.5-m) poles together,

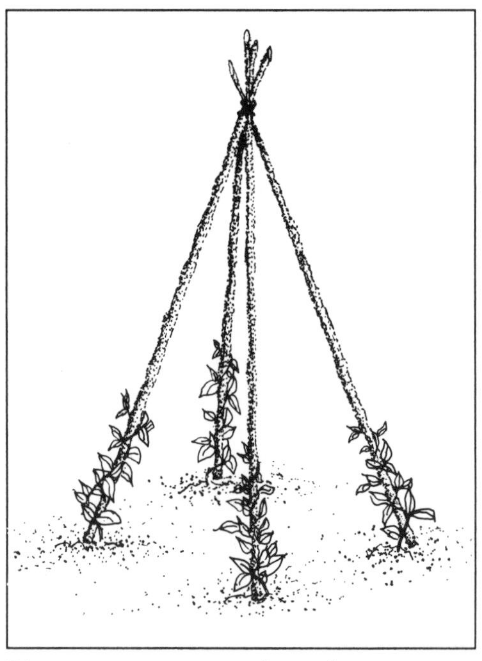

Teepees are easy to make and maximize garden space.

spread out the free ends and push them into the soil, forming a tripod. Plant two or three seeds at each pole. Pole beans will produce over a long period of time right through until fall.

Scarlet runner beans resemble pole beans, but the flowers are a lovely red color and the plants have lush, dark green foliage. Scarlet runner beans are often used as a temporary ornamental screen to shade a porch or patio, with the added advantage of providing fresh beans to eat. Although the plants are perennial in mild climates, they are grown as an annual here. The plants require support similar to that used for pole beans. The vines will twine counterclockwise up a pole, but they may need a bit of encouragement to get started on their way. Scarlet runners are usually sown direct, but to get a head start, they may be started indoors four weeks before it will be warm enough to set them out.

When the flowers drop without forming pods, it is often caused by cool weather. It may happen because the flowers were not fertilized: during cool, overcast weather the bees do not fly. Bumblebees and birds can also knock the flowers off. The pods are flat, slightly fuzzy and 6 to 8 inches (15 to 20 cm) long. The plants are heavy producers.

Harvest Time: Beans can be harvested from early summer through the fall, depending on the variety and successive plantings.

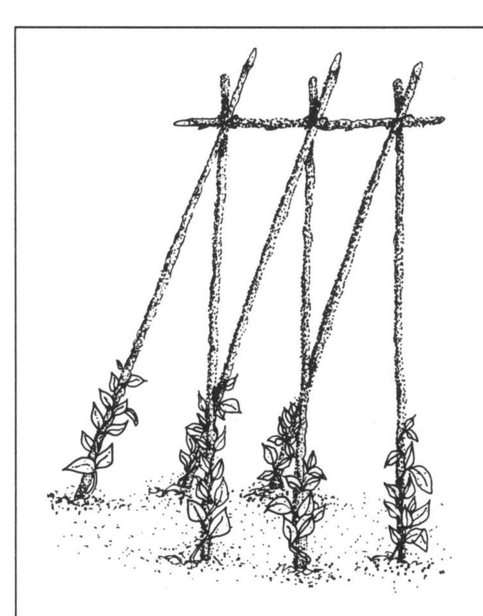

Staking is necessary for tall varieties of beans.

Height: Bush beans are less than 1 foot (30 cm) and pole and runner beans are 6 feet (2 m) or more.

Light and Soil: All beans require full sun and warm temperatures. The soil should be well drained and fertile with a pH from 6.5 to 7.0.

How to Grow: Beans are sown directly once the soil has warmed, mid-May to early June. For proper germination the soil should be 50°F (10°C). Sow the seeds 1 1/2 inches (3.5 cm) deep and 2 inches (5 cm) apart. Within double rows, space the plants 6 inches (15 cm) apart.

Leave a path 18 inches (45 cm) to 2 feet (60 cm) wide between single or double rows.

In colder areas, start the plants in paper pots indoors, taking care not to disturb the roots when they are transplanted. Bush beans may be covered with a plastic tunnel to extend the growing season.

Water is very important, especially during flowering and when the pods are forming. Plants that are under stress will yield less and will be more susceptible to disease. Try mulching the plants.

Harvesting: Pick beans often, usually every second day. The pods should not look full, so that you can see the individual beans. Old bean pods get stringy and they are not very appetizing to eat. If a pod is missed and it has become too old to eat, pull it off. Once the plant has mature seed pods, it will stop producing more beans.

Be careful when picking the beans. Support the plant with your other hand so it will not be damaged; it is very easy to pull the whole plant out of the ground by giving the pod a tug. This is particularly true for bush beans.

Storage: Beans are tastiest when they are eaten soon after they have been picked, but they will keep for a week in the refrigerator if they are put in a plastic bag. Beans should be blanched for three minutes before they are frozen, or they may also be processed in canning jars. Pickled beans are tasty, and when they are packed whole and upright in the jar they look very attractive.

Pests and Diseases: Beans are attacked by aphids, weevils, flea beetles, cutworms, slugs, thrips and wireworms. Some aphids that attack beans spread a virus from plant to plant so it is important to control them. For more information on these pests, see chapter six, Pests and Diseases.

Beans are susceptible to many diseases: root rots, bacterial blights, fungal leaf spots, viruses, molds and rust. Always practice crop rotation, clean up all debris after the crop is harvested, avoid overfertilizing, do not plant the plants too close together and control aphids.

Rust spores blow in the wind and are transferred as you move between the plants. They cause reddish spots on the leaves and pods. Plant beans that are more resistant to rust (bush beans are more rust-resistant than pole beans) and rotate the crop. Sanitation will help to stop its spread by removing and destroying infected leaves and pods. Never work around the plants when they are wet.

White and **gray mold** are similar diseases. White mold can cause damping-off of seedlings and both can cause a fluffy growth on pods and stems. The diseases are prevalent during wet springs and the plants will often die. Both white and gray mold require dying tissue in order to grow. The disease often starts at the bottom of the bean, on the remains of the flower or an old leaf. Frequently beans that are touching the ground become moldy because the disease remains in the soil on dead organic material. This is a disease that primarily affects bush beans in wet seasons. To control white and gray mold, rotate the crop, avoid over-fertilizing and overhead watering, and do not crowd the plants.

Varieties: 'Blue Lake Bush' is a tasty older variety. A newer one on the market, 'Venture Blue Lake Bush', is a similar bean; it will germinate in cooler soils and is very productive. 'Royal Burgundy' is a purple-podded bush bean which grows on a sturdy plant. The pods turn green when they are cooked. 'Golden Rocky' is a Dutch-bred yellow-podded bush bean.

'Kentucky Wonder' and 'Blue Lake' are favorite old-fashioned varieties of pole beans and are available anywhere. 'Kentucky Wonder Wax' is a pale yellow, truly waxy bean. 'Violet Podded Stringless' from Territorial Seeds will sprout when the soil is still cool, which is a real advantage when growing beans.

Scarlet runner beans are not usually sold by variety but just as "Scarlet Runner Bean."

Hint: After the bean crop is finished, cut the plants off at ground level, leaving the roots in the ground. This leaves the nitrogen-rich nodules on the roots to provide nitrogen for the next crop.

Grow morning glories and scarlet runner beans together. They will intertwine and be very attractive. The morning glories will not interfere with picking the bean pods.

BEANS, BROAD *Vicia faba*

Broad or fava beans are treated differently from pole and bush beans because they grow well during our long, cool springs and they will do well into summer if the weather is not too hot. Broad beans are much beloved by the English and grow very well on the West Coast.

Harvest Time: Early summer.

Height: 3 to 5 feet (1 to 1.5 m).

Light and Soil: Broad beans need to be planted in the full sun. The soil should be well drained with a pH from 5.5 to 6.5.

How to Grow: Broad beans are seeded in March as soon as the soil can be worked. They do not need to be fertilized if the soil is fertile, but some

6-8-6 could be applied when the seeds are sown. Watering is usually not necessary. Sow the seeds 1 1/2 inches (4 cm) deep and 5 inches (12 cm) apart. Plant in single or double rows and leave a 2 1/2-foot (75-cm) path. The plants are partially freestanding but will benefit from some support. Three-foot (1-m), twiggy branches pushed into the ground will give the plants support as they grow.
Harvesting: The young beans can be eaten pod and all, but once the pods are well developed and the shape of the beans can be seen through the flat-sided pod, shell them and cook the bean seeds. The pods are fairly fat and about 8 to 10 inches (20 to 25 cm) in length. The beans should never be allowed to get too large or they will become tough. The scar on the bean seed should be green, not black.
Storage: Young beans can be refrigerated for up to a week in a plastic bag or they can be blanched and frozen for later use. Mature beans can be dried to use in soups.
Pests and Diseases: The number-one pest on broad beans is the **bean aphid**, or "black fly" (an aphid is not a fly, but black fly is its common name). When the first few aphids are spotted, nip off the top 4 or 5 inches (7 or 12 cm) of growth. This will only work if the plants have reached full height when the aphids first attack. If the aphids are deprived of the succulent new growth, they usually do not become a problem. There is a story about an elderly gardener who was never troubled with black aphids on his broad beans. When he was asked how he did it he replied, "I remove the tops the day before they arrive." A lot of gardening is like that. With experience it becomes instinctive when it's the right time to do something such as outfoxing the aphids.

Soap spray is effective on these aphids or you can rub them off with your fingers. They usually congregate on the tender tip growth, but also watch the underside of the leaves. The plants are usually fairly free of other problems.
Varieties: 'Windsor Beans' or 'Broad Windsor' are a well-known old variety that is worth growing today. 'Long Windsor Pod' is another one of the Windsor-type beans grown for its longer pods. Sometimes broad beans are sold in packages simply labeled broad bean, without a variety.
Hint: In warmer areas like the coast, sow broad beans in the fall and cover the plants with Reemay. This will give an early harvest most years, but it does depend on the winter weather. Some years you may lose the crop.

BEETS *Beta vulgaris*

Garden beets are cultivated for their roots but the tender foliage is also eaten as a green. Beet roots may be round or long and slender, and the color can vary from deep red to yellow, white or reddish purple. Beets are a cool-weather crop and tend to bolt when it gets too hot.

It wasn't until the 16th century that beet roots were eaten, although its close relative, Swiss chard, was eaten by the Greeks and Romans. Near Winnipeg, where I grew up, sugar beets are grown. They look not unlike a large rutabaga and each beet yields about a tablespoon of sugar. It takes a lot of beets to fill a bag of sugar. Mangel-wurzels or mangel are beets used as cattle feed.

Harvest Time: Late spring through fall.

Height: 6 to 10 inches (15 to 25 cm).

Light and Soil: Beets will grow in most soils but they need a pH of 6.5 to 7.5. Dig in some well-rotted compost and add a basic fertilizer like 6-8-6. Beets are usually grown in full sun but they will tolerate some light shade. The seeds will germinate best if the soil temperature is 50°F (10°C). If the soil temperature is below 54°F (7°C) the seeds will not germinate.

How to Grow: Beets are hardy and the seeds can be direct-sown 2 to 3 weeks before the last frost date. The seeds can be sown indoors 4 weeks before planting out, but the seedling must be handled carefully to avoid breaking the tap root. Sow the seeds 1/2 inch (1 cm) deep and 1/2 inch (1 cm) apart. To aid germination, soak the seeds for an hour before they are planted, but germination is often spotty. The rows are more productive if they are planted in bands three or four rows deep with an 18-inch (45-cm) path between each banded row, rather than in single rows. Beets require adequate water and the plants can be mulched if necessary.

The corky beet seed is really a small fruit and usually yields two or three plants. Use the extra tiny seedlings from each seed to fill in the gaps; the extra seedlings can also be snipped off with scissors to give the plant the best chance to grow undisturbed.

When the beets are an inch (2.5 cm) in diameter, thin the plants to 4 inches (10 cm) apart by removing every other beet.

Harvesting: At the beginning of the season steam the tender beet thinnings or use them in salads. The next thinning will yield tiny beets, a wonderful taste treat. The mature beet root will be almost all above the ground; they keep fairly well in the ground unless the temperature gets too hot. In the fall beets can be mulched and left in the ground for storage.

When cooking beets, always leave an inch (2.5 cm) or so of the leaf stalk on the root to prevent the beets from bleeding. Small beets will cook in 20 minutes in boiling water but larger, older beets may take almost an hour to cook. Once they are cooked, plunge the beets into cold water, cut off the stem and the skin will slip off easily. Use a fork to hold the beet while you peel it unless you don't mind having red hands for awhile (although a couple of washings will remove the dye).

Storage: Beets can be stored for several months in a cool, moist place. Remove the leaves, leaving several inches (cm) of the stem, and layer the beets in dry peat or sand so they are not touching each other. Beets may also be frozen, processed in jars and pickled.

Problems: Woody beets can result from water stress or inadequate thinning. **Early bolting** is caused by water and heat stress, late thinning, or from seeding too early. **Split** or **hairy roots** may be from too much manure, a rocky site or transplanting the seedlings too late.

Black heart shows up in the root as black spots inside the beet or dry, hard spots on the surface. It may be caused by a boron deficiency, which is more prevalant in alkaline soils especially when the plants have lacked water. A soil test is recommended. To add boron to the soil, dig in some compost or manure and use a fertilizer that lists boron as a trace element.

Pests and Disease: Leaf miner is the most frequent pest problem on beets. The foliage takes on a silvery look as the maggot feeds inside the leaf. A heavy leaf miner infestation reduces the plant's ability to photosynthesize and it will stunt the growth. A little damage will not affect the root, but the leaf will no longer be edible. There are several generations of the miner over the summer. The adult fly lays her eggs on the underside of the leaves and the maggot hatches and burrows into the leaf. Remove the affected leaves before the larva matures and drops to the ground to pupate. Practice rigorous weed control; the miner also infests lambs quarters and chickweed. Eggs can be rubbed off the leaves when they are spotted. If the leaf miner fly has been a problem in the past, as soon as possible cover the crop with Reemay. The fly overwinters in the soil but if the crop has been rotated there should not be flies in the soil where the new crop has been planted. It is always a good idea to check under the cloth to be sure an insect hasn't sneaked in.

Scab can be a problem. It is compounded because beets grow best in soils with a higher pH, which also increases the incidence of the disease. It is the same disease that affects potatoes. The crop is still edible, however, as it only affects the skin, and beets are skinned before eating.

To help prevent scab, grow a green manure crop over the winter and incorporate it into the soil in the spring. Rotate the beet crop. Avoid growing beets where potatoes have grown if they have had scab.
Varieties: 'Detroit Dark Red' is an older variety which is still a top one to grow. 'Detroit Supreme' was bred from 'Detroit Dark Red' and was chosen as an All-American Selection. One of my favorites is 'Little Ball', an older variety that produces small round beets. 'Winter Keeper' is a good beet to sow mid-July on the coast; it will keep in the ground through the winter if it is mulched. 'Burpee Golden' is a yellow color, somewhat of a surprise if you picture beets as red. When it is cooked it still tastes like a beet.

BROCCOLI and SPROUTING BROCCOLI *Brassica oleracea*

Broccoli is a member of the cabbage, kale, crucifer or brassica family and its wild parent, *B. oleracea*, is also the parent of cauliflower, cabbage, kale, Brussels sprouts and other kale crops. Through cultivation, different characteristics have been developed. Broccoli is grown for its dense flowering head that tops a heavy edible stem which is closely related to cauliflower. At one time they were classed together as one vegetable and in old English it was called sprout colli-flower. It finally evolved that cauliflower forms heads and broccoli forms sprouts. Broccoli is a cool-season annual that can withstand some frost.

Sprouting broccoli looks like the ancestor of today's broccoli. It has edible shoots but it doesn't have a large central head. It is grown in Europe more than in North America, but the interest in the vegetable is increasing, particularly with people who come from Europe and remember eating it when they lived there. It is a very hardy vegetable that grows well in the Pacific Northwest. Sow the seeds in July and the crop will be ready to harvest by mid-February to March.
Harvest Time: Harvest broccoli from late spring through fall. Sprouting broccoli is picked in the early spring.
Height: 2 to 3 feet (60 to 90 cm).
Light and Soil: Broccoli does best in well-cultivated soil that has had compost or other organic matter dug into it and has good drainage. Broccoli will grow in poorer soils but will never attain large heads. It will tolerate light shade. Feed it with a balanced fertilizer like 6-8-6 and side-dress when the central head starts to form. This will promote growth of the side shoots which will become a good size and extend the season. Side-dress again when the top is harvested.

How to Grow: Plants can be direct-seeded from April through to mid-July. Transplants may be started inside, or in a cold frame or a greenhouse, in March and transplanted out in April. By sowing varieties with different maturity dates you can extend the season further. Sow three seeds separately, 1/2 inch (1 cm) deep with 18 inches (45 cm) intervals between plants and 2 feet (60 cm) between rows. The three seedlings are thinned to the strongest plant when the first set of true leaves are showing. Keep the plants well watered and mulch during hot spells.
Harvesting: The top floret is cut with 4 to 6 inches (10 to 15 cm) of stem. The green head should be tight. If it is left too long the plant will flower. Side shoots will develop after the central head is removed. They will be smaller but just as tasty.
Storage: Broccoli can be stored in the refrigerator for three days, or frozen.
Problems: Hollow or corky stems indicate a boron deficiency. See the Beets entry for remedial measures.
Pests and Diseases: Many diseases attack kale crops, including downy mildew and clubroot. To reduce the incidence of disease, increase the air circulation around the plants, rotate the kale family crops, and observe good garden sanitation. Where kale crops are grown keep the pH at a level of 7.0 by adding lime to the soil.

Aphids, cutworms, cabbage loopers, slugs and wireworms may be a problem in kale crops. *Bacillus thuringiensis* (BT) is not always effective on kale crops because they contain an ingredient that inhibits the bacteria that attacks the caterpillars. For more information on these problems, see chapter six, Pests and Diseases.
Varieties: 'Watham 29' is a standard variety that is harvested in the fall. 'GreenValiant' and 'Shogun' produce large heads that are very compact and are both good choices. Sprouting broccoli is often sold as Purple or White Sprouting.
Hint: If you have access to seaweed, apply it as a mulch or dig it into the soil before spring planting. It seems to help keep the plants free from root maggots.

BRUSSELS SPROUTS *Brassica oleracea*

Although the first written mention of Brussels sprouts was in the 1500s, this vegetable was not well known outside Belgium and France until around 150 years ago, when it made its way to North America. It is named for the city of Brussels in Belgium, near where the vegetable was likely developed.

Brussels sprouts have a sturdy stem and at each leaf axil a small sprout, resembling a miniature cabbage, forms. Although the crop is not harvested until fall, the plants require a long, cool growing season. Brussels sprouts do well on the coast because of the cooler summers.

Harvest Time: Pick the sprouts after the first frost in the fall and on through winter as they are needed. Brussels sprouts are hardy and they will survive most of our winters on the coast. They will usually not be harmed by a hard frost.

Height: 2 feet (60 cm).

Light and Soil: Plant Brussels sprouts in full sun in average garden soil that has been amended with compost or other organic matter. Brussels sprouts will also do well in heavy soil that has more clay.

How to Grow: Sow seeds in the garden the end of May or by the beginning of June, because the plants have a long growing season. If seedlings are grown, set them out by the beginning of July and space the plants 2 feet (60 cm) apart. The plants will need a continued supply of nutrients and water throughout the summer. Pull off any yellowed leaves in the fall, but leave the green ones. They help to protect the sprouts when the fall rains make the outer leaves on the sprouts rather messy.

Harvesting: The sprouts are ready to eat when they are an inch (2.5 cm) in diameter. They are removed by twisting the sprout. Do not expect the sprouts picked during the winter to look like those in the grocery stores, but the flavor will be tops. The rain will make the outer leaves slimy, but simply remove them.

Storage: The sprouts are best left on the plant on the coast. In colder areas the whole plant, bare-rooted, can be brought into a cold, frost-free place and harvested as needed. Brussels sprouts can be frozen.

Pests and Diseases: Occasionally, aphids, loopers, and wireworms can be a problem with Brussels sprouts but generally the plants are trouble free.

Varieties: An old standby is 'Jade Cross', an early-maturing variety that is good for a home garden. 'Long Island Improved' has medium-sized sprouts and is a good choice for the home garden. 'Aries' F1 is very cold hardy and will withstand harder frosts. 'Captain Marvel' F1 has very firm sprouts and tolerates the cold well.

Hint: Plant Brussels sprouts where you will have easy access to them in the winter.

CABBAGE *Brassica olereacea*

Cabbage is a cool-season biennial that forms heads of various shapes and sizes. The color may vary from green to metallic blue and purple. Cabbages average 2 to 6 pounds (1 to 3 kg). Cabbage with its overlapping leaves repels rain and does well on the coast with its cool summers and mild winters. It can withstand some frost and supplies flavorful greens through most winters.

Cabbage is native to the south coast of England, Denmark and the north coast of France. Jacques Cartier introduced it to Canada in 1669, but it wasn't eaten in Great Britain until the 1850s, when it was introduced into Scotland by Cromwell. The cabbage is the wild ancestor that all the kale crops were bred from: broccoli, Brussels sprouts, turnips, kohlrabi, kales and ornamental cabbages and kales.

The ornamental cabbages and kales are attractive and they are worthy of a place in the flower garden and winter flower beds. In fact, all varieties of ornamental cabbage are edible. The looser heads of the ornamental kales withstand the rains on the coast better than the ornamental cabbage varieties, which tend to trap the rain.

Harvest Time: Cabbage is harvested from summer through early winter.

Height: 8 to 18 inches (20 to 45 cm).

Light and Soil: Cabbages will grow in light shade to full sun. They need a fertile soil and will benefit if some compost or other organic matter is added to the soil. Cabbage grows best when the pH is 6.0 to 7.0.

How to Grow: Several varieties of cabbage have been developed to mature in early spring, summer, fall and winter.

The early varieties are seeded mid-April through June. Sow the seeds with 1/2 inch (1 cm) of soil and sprinkle some 6-8-6 along the rows at planting time. Thin the plants when they are 4 to 5 inches (10 to 13 cm) tall, spacing them 14 to 16 inches (35 to 40 cm) apart. Seedlings may be started earlier to plant out in mid-April—or earlier if they are protected in cold frames or with cloches. Early cabbage is less hardy and does not hold up as well as the late varieties. Succession plantings will give a continued supply of fresh cabbage through the summer. Do not plant more than you can use at any one time, because the early cabbages do not keep as well as the winter varieties.

Winter or late varieties take almost twice as long to mature as the spring varieties. Sow them in early June through the first week in July for fall and early winter harvesting. Once the winter cabbages are established, side-dress them with a fertilizer that is high in nitrogen.

Mulch with compost or other organic material to help conserve moisture and keep down the weeds. Mulch or hand weeding is better than hoeing, which must be done with care as the roots are shallow.
Harvesting: Pick cabbage when the heads are well formed and firm. If the heads are left too long they tend to crack. If the roots and 3 inches (7 cm) or so of stem are left after the head is harvested, the plant will grow several small heads from the dormant buds. These will be tender and delicious. The outer leaves of the winter cabbage may become slimy with the winter rains, but once they are removed you will find a good firm head underneath.
Storage: Summer cabbages will keep three to four weeks in the refrigerator. Excess cabbage can be preserved as sauerkraut. The heads of the late-maturing cabbage can be stored in a cool, frost-free place with high humidity for 3 to 4 months. The late cabbage is moderately frost tolerant and may be left in the garden until needed most winters.
Pests and Diseases: Imported cabbageworm and loopers, flea beetle, cabbage maggot, clubroot and other fungus diseases may be a problem. These insects and diseases which affect all the kale crops are discussed in chapter six, Pests and Diseases.
Varieties: Early maturing varieties, such as 'Golden Acre' and 'Derby Day', a 'Golden Acre' type, are a deep green and are mildly flavored. 'Ruby Ball' F1 is a dark purple cabbage that keeps well in the garden even after it has matured. 'Red Rodan' is a late variety that holds well in the garden until late winter. 'Winterstar' F1 is a savoy type and a good choice for winter growing as it is hardy and has a good flavor. Savoy means the leaves have wavy edges; the term applies not only to cabbage but to any leaf that has wavy leaf margins.

CABBAGE, ORIENTAL or CHINESE *Brassica rapa*

The name Oriental or Chinese cabbage can apply to a number of different plants, but they are usually of two types, heading and nonheading varieties. Heading types include wong bok, napa cabbage and Chinese celery. Nonheading types are bok choy and Chinese mustard cabbage. The plants are grown like cabbage but the flavor is generally milder.
Harvest Times: Chinese cabbages are harvested in summer through to winter.
Height: From 6 to 18 inches (15 to 46 cm) depending on the variety.
Light and Soil: Chinese cabbage does best in a rich, moist soil with lots

of added organic matter. They will grow in light shade to full sun.

How to Grow: The heading Chinese cabbage is very sensitive to day length, and fluctuating temperatures can cause the plants to bolt. The plants grow best when the temperatures are in 60 to 63°F, (15 to 17°C), and they need to have good growing conditions— warmth, moisture and nutrients—so the plants can grow quickly. It is not a good idea to plant them early in the spring; wait until June or July. Direct-sow the seeds; thin when they are 4 inches (10 cm) tall, spacing them 12 to 18 inches (30 to 45 cm) apart. Give the plants fertilizer, such as 6-8-6, at sowing and side-dress after the first month. Transplanting is not very successful unless the plants are small, because they do not like to have their roots disturbed.

The nonheading varieties may be sown in the early spring and again at the end of July, for a fall harvest. The nonheading varieties are particularly suitable for small gardens because they can be harvested by the leaf.

Harvesting: Heading varieties are harvested by cutting off the whole head. Nonheading varieties can be harvested whole or by the leaf.

Problems: Boron deficiency can cause hollow stems and browning of the pith, with excessive leaf curling. Sometimes the plants fail to form heads. To correct the problem, add manure or compost to the soil and use fertilizers that contain boron as a trace element.

Pests and Diseases: Pests and diseases that attack cabbage also attack Chinese cabbage: aphids, cabbage maggot, cutworms, cabbage looper, imported cabbageworm and flea beetles. Cover the crop with Reemay or other floating mulch to prevent flea beetles and the cabbageworm butterfly from laying its eggs. Diseases include clubroot, downy mildew and other fungus and bacterial diseases. Please see the Pests and Disease chapter for further information on these problems.

Varieties: 'Nerva' F1 is an early heading variety and it is bolt resistant. 'China Express' F1 is a later heading variety that will take some frost in the fall. 'Tah Tsai' is a dark-leafed nonheading variety that has spoon-shaped leaves and white stems (a good addition to stir-fry dishes). Bok choi looks like Swiss chard but only the inner leaves and stems are harvested. Pak choi has slimmer stems than bok choi and both of them are nonheading types.

CABBAGE and KALE, ORNAMENTAL *Brassica oleracea*

These hardy plants are usually grown for their ornamental value, although you will often see them for sale as a vegetable, especially in the Chinese markets. The leaves make a colorful addition in salads and are used to decorate plates. If you are using them for winter color in the garden, start them mid-June through July. The colors are better when they develop during colder weather. The plants will not survive hard frosts.

The seeds are sold as a mixture of colors or a single variety. The kales that do not form heads will stand up much better in the winter rains; the head-forming varieties hold the water in the leaves and rot.

For cultural requirements and pest and disease control, see the sections under Cabbage.

CARROT *Daucus carota* var. *sativus*

Carrots are biennials that are grown as annuals for the tasty root. If you have seen a carrot flower the summer after it was seeded, you won't be surprised to learn that the pretty weed Queen Anne's lace is so closely related that it has the same genus and species designation as carrots.

Carrots have been in the medicinal pharmacopeia of man since early times. By the 1300s it had spread from the Mediterranean, where it is native, to the rest of Europe; but it is only in this century that the carrot root has developed and improved to where it is edible as a raw vegetable. Carrots are naturally very diverse, coming in all shapes and sizes, from long and slender to short and squat.

Harvest Time: Carrots are harvested throughout the summer to late fall.
Height: 8 to 10 inches (20 to 25 cm).
Light and Soil: Carrots are usually planted in full sun but they can withstand light shade. They require a well-dug, deep, fertile soil with a pH of 6.5 to 7. Feed with a balanced fertilizer like 6-8-6. If you want to add manure, plan to do it the previous fall; it must be well-rotted or the roots will split and be covered with a surplus of tiny roots. Roots will also split if the soil is excessively stony. If the soil is rocky or is not very deep, try planting the stubbier varieties of carrots. You can also build a raised bed or dig a trench the length of the row and fill it with good soil. The trench should be about 3 inches (7 cm) wide and deep enough to accommodate the variety of carrot you are growing.
How to Grow: Sow seeds at weekly intervals from mid-April through mid-July for a continual supply of carrots. In milder areas, carrots can be sown by the end of March. As well as weekly sowings, use different varieties, such as 'Earlybird Nantes', which matures in 50 days, and

'Royal Chantenay', which takes 60 days to mature, to stretch out the harvest.

Sow the seeds thinly, 1/2 inch (1 cm) deep, and thin the plants to 1 1/2 inches (4 cm) apart. Thinning is tedious but important if the roots are to grow. Rows can be single, but planting in multiple banded rows works well. Keep the soil moist–you might cover the row with plastic until the seeds germinate. It is most important to prevent the soil from drying out when the roots are forming; if it dries out at this stage, the plant will be under stress and it will not be as sweet or tasty. Also keep the crop well watered during the summer heat.

Harvesting: If the carrots were sown thinly you will not have to thin until they are little-finger size. Pull every second plant, leaving the rest to mature. Young carrots are the most flavorful; older ones tend to crack and there is more time for the carrot rust fly maggot to invade the root.

Storage: Late-maturing carrots can be left in the ground in the fall if the soil is well drained. In colder areas mulch the area heavily to prevent the ground from freezing. Carrots will keep in the refrigerator for two to three weeks in a plastic bag or they can be stored in a cold room, just above freezing, with high humidity, for three to four months. Carrots can be frozen, preserved in jars and pickled.

Problems: Forked roots are caused by too much nitrogen in the soil or fresh manure. If the soil is stony it may cause the roots to split. Splitting can also be caused by uneven moisture; do not allow the soil to dry out too much and then water heavily.

Deformed roots can result from not thinning the plants, heavy soil that the roots have trouble pushing through, or stones.

Pests and Diseases: Wireworms, cutworms and nematodes may attack carrots. For details on how to combat these pests refer to chapter six, Pests and Diseases. Carrot rust fly and several diseases–aster yellows, white mold, and rusty root–are detailed below.

Carrot rust fly is the number-one pest of carrots on the south coast of B.C. It has two to three generations over the summer and also attacks celery, parsley and parsnips. The adult, a small fly with yellow legs, lays its eggs on the soil beside the plant and the maggots feed on the root. Young plants may be killed and mature plants can become unappetizing, with tunneled roots. The pupae overwinter in the soil. Floating mulches, sanitation, rotation and weed control are the best defence. Put plants that are infected with larvae into the garbage and don't leave them sitting around in the garden. Do not leave thinnings around because the scent attracts the carrot rust fly. Slightly hill up the soil, covering the exposed shoulder of the root; this helps to discourage the fly, as it lays the eggs on the exposed root. The best control is to use a floating mulch like Reemay or Agronet. Leave enough slack so the growing plants do not have to push up the mulch.

Aster yellows is a disease that is transmitted by leaf hoppers. Its symptoms are a yellowing of the foliage and new shoots that are twisted, with a witch's-broom appearance. It is more common in the Interior. Rigorously remove weeds, which are an alternate host for leaf hoppers, and destroy infected plants.

White mold causes a watery rot with lots of white mold in evidence. Hard round black particles (sclerotia) will be noticeable in the mold. The sclerotia drop to the ground to infect the next crop of carrots, so rotating crops helps to prevent reinfection.

Rusty root may be a problem during wet years. The small side roots turn reddish orange and die back. If you live in an area where the water table is high, grow carrots in raised beds and increase the space between the plants.

Varieties: 'Mokum' F1 is a top-flavored carrot—a must for eating fresh out of the garden. 'Baby Finger Nantes' and 'Baby Orange' are two varieties of the baby carrots that have become so popular in the last few years. At maturity they are only a few inches (7 cm) long. 'Royal Chantenay' and 'Orange Sherbet' are two excellent carrots.

CAULIFLOWER *Brassica oleracea*

Cauliflower is a cool-weather vegetable that looks like a loose leaf cabbage before it matures; its seedlings resemble other kale crops. Cauliflower is native to the Mediterranean region and it is an ancient vegetable. By the Middle Ages cold-hardy plants were grown in Europe.

The plants take up a lot of space in a garden but may be interspaced with lettuce, radish and other fast-growing crops. By the time the cauliflower has grown enough to shade the other crops, it will have been harvested. The edible part of the cauliflower is a tight cluster of flower buds, or curds. If the plant is left too long, the curds start to separate and the head is no longer smooth, although the buds do not flower the way broccoli will if it's left unharvested.

The self-blanching varieties have leaves that naturally curve over the plants, but to be truly blanched even the self-blanching varieties should be covered. To blanch the head, break some of the inner leaves so they protect the developing flower head, or tie the leaves loosely over the head. You can use a nylon stocking to tie the leaves or slip it over the head and leaves. Unblanched heads are a rather unappetizing brown but are still edible. The purple varieties do not need blanching and seem to have fewer pest problems. Cauliflower will withstand some frost.

Harvest Time: Cauliflower is harvested from early summer through winter. The early-planted crops are harvested in the summer, later-planted varieties in the fall and fall-planted cauliflower overwinters and is harvested in the early spring.

Height: 1 to 2 feet (30 to 60 cm).

Light and Soil: Cauliflowers need a rich, well-drained soil with a pH of 6.5 to 7.0. If clubroot is a problem, keep the pH at 7.0 to help control the disease. To enrich the soil dig compost in when the soil is being prepared in the spring. The soil should be well drained. Grow the plants in full sun or light shade.

How to Grow: Cauliflower plants must grow quickly so they will need to be well fertilized and have good soil conditions. Use an all-purpose fertilizer like 6-8-6 when the seeds are directly sown in the ground or set out as transplants. The kale crops transplant well; the early ones are usually transplanted but the later ones are direct-seeded. Top-dress after a month with a fertilizer that is high in nitrogen. Do not let the seeded area or transplants dry out, and mulch the plants to help retain the moisture. Transplants may be started, preferably in individual containers from mid-February until mid-March, about 4 to 6 weeks before they are set out.

Direct sowing of early varieties starts the end of April. Sow several seeds 1/2 inch (1 cm) deep every 20 inches (50 cm). The rows should be spaced 2 feet (60 cm) apart. When the seedlings are 4 inches (10 cm) high, thin out all but the strongest plants. Be careful when weeding, because the roots are shallow. There are varieties available for all seasons including some overwintering varieties offered by Territorial Seeds for growing on the coast. Start transplants in mid-July because it is usually too hot to directly sow the seeds. Transplants are set out in the first two weeks in August. They will not do well every winter, as about one out of every four years it is too cold.

Harvesting: Cut off the head, including some of the leaves, when the head is still tight and the curds are just barely beginning to separate. If the cut stock is left, sometimes small heads will form from side shoots.

Storage: Fresh cauliflower can be stored in the refrigerator for one to two weeks, wrapped in plastic. Extra heads may be blanched and frozen, or pickled.

Problems: Cauliflower with boron deficiencies will have brown, bitter heads. Compost and manure, as well as some fertilizers, contain boron; check the trace elements on the package. These are the safest ways to get more boron into the soil.

Small heads are caused by stress from cold, drought or heat.

Pests and Diseases: All the brassicas are affected by the same pests and diseases: aphids, cutworms, flea beetles, slugs, cabbageworms and wireworms. They are also subject to several fungus diseases, including white rot, leaf spots, downy mildew and clubroot. Refer to chapter six, Pests and Diseases, for more details on these pests.

Varieties: 'Alpha' varieties, such as 'Early Alpha' and 'Alpha Paloma', are early varieties that may be started indoors as transplants and moved to the garden in April under cloches. If several varieties are planted, the season for early cauliflower will be extended. 'White Rock' and 'White Sails' are two midseason varieties. 'Burgundy Queen' is a midseason variety that tolerates heat. 'Purple Cape' is an attractive, purple overwintering variety. 'Armado Spring' Plus is a package that contains an assortment of winter cauliflowers, including 'Armado Quick', 'Armado May' and 'Armado April'.

CELERY *Apium graveolens* var. *dulce*

Celery is another biennial that is grown as an annual. Because the stocks were bitter and tough, it was used medicinally and as a flavoring long before it was eaten as a vegetable. It is likely native to the Mediterranean area and its wild ancestor, smallage, has spread to Europe and Asia where it grows in marshy areas.

Celery does well on the West Coast, with its long cool summers. It has the reputation of being difficult to grow, but the secret is never to let it suffer stress from drought or heat. Home-grown celery will have a stronger flavor than store-bought, and unblanched stalks will have a stronger flavor than those that are blanched.

Harvest Time: Celery is harvested in the late summer through fall. In mild coastal areas it can be harvested stalk by stalk through most winters.

Height: 15 to 18 inches (43 to 50 cm).

Light and Soil: Celery grows in full sun, but it will also tolerate light shade. It needs rich, well-prepared soil that has had rotted manure or compost dug into it so it will hold moisture well. Celery grows best when the pH is between 5.2 and 6.5.

How to Grow: Celery requires a lot of water, and it is a heavy feeder. Fertilize at planting time with 6-8-6 and side-dress with a high-nitrogen fertilizer once the plants are established. Transplants can be started in March for mid-May planting. Germinate the seeds in a cool place, 60 to 70°F (15 to 20°C). Do not put the transplants out until the nights have warmed up. Nighttime temperatures should not be below 55 to 60°F (12 to 15°C). Young seedlings that are exposed to the cold may bolt. Bolting is the premature flowering of a plant, usually caused by stress. Transplants can be put in a cold frame at the end of April. Keep the plants well watered and fertilize with a liquid feed every two weeks until they are 4 inches (10 cm) tall. Thin them to 6 inches (15 cm) apart when they are about 5 inches (12 cm) tall. Seeds can be directly sown 1/4 inch (.5 cm) deep from early May through June. Keep the soil moist while they germinate.

Many varieties grown now are self-blanching, such as 'Golden' and Stokes 'Golden Plume'. The green varieties that are available now are tender and blanching is no longer necessary. But if you wish to blanch the stems, wrap them about two weeks before harvesting with freezer paper, or place boards snugly up against the row on either side of the plants. Soil can also be used to hill up around the plants, but it is hard to wash out of the stalks when they are harvested. Open-ended clay pipes or milk cartons can be placed around individual plants; they work well and are easy to use.

Mulching is a good practice around celery. It helps to conserve water and keep the soil evenly moist.

Harvesting: Individual stalks can be harvested as needed, or the whole plant can be picked by cutting it off at ground level.

Storage: Celery can be wrapped in plastic and stored for two weeks in the refrigerator. On the coast leave the plants in the garden and harvest as the stalks are needed.

Problems: **Bitter stalks** can be caused by stress from lack of water or nutrients. They will also become bitter if they are too mature when they are harvested. Plants may bolt if it is too cold when they are first transplanted into the garden. Bolting is also caused by other stresses, such as prolonged hot, dry weather or lack of moisture.

Pests and Diseases: Aphids, carrot rust fly, slugs and cutworms can attack celery. For the control of these pests refer to chapter six, Pests and

Diseases (carrot rust fly is detailed in the Carrots entry). Celery is susceptible to several fungus diseases, which can usually be avoided with crop rotation, good garden sanitation and proper fertilization.
Varieties: 'Utah 5270' Improved is a dark green, tender celery that is grown commercially. It is tender without blanching. 'Golden' and 'Golden Plume' are both self-blanching.

CORN *Zea mays*

Corn is a New World native that was and still is known as maize to most of the world, with the exception of North Americans. It is an ancient crop that was first cultivated by the Incas of Peru and later Mexicans and the North American Indians. Columbus returned to Europe with tales of corn grown for flour. Cow corn is still grown as animal feed and is likely similar to the early corn that was ground into flour. Sweet corn for fresh eating was not developed until this century, when a lot of breeding has been done to develop new varieties that stay sweet for more than a few hours after harvest.

The genes in the old corn varieties are important to improve the disease resistance of this agricultural crop. A primitive perennial variety was recently discovered in Mexico. Someday, our whole way of growing corn may be revolutionized.

Corn is a warm-season, annual member of the grass family Gramineae. The three types of corn that are often grown in a vegetable garden—sweet corn, *Z. mays* var. *rugosa*, popcorn, *Z. mays* var. *everta*, and ornamental corn, *Z. mays* var. *indurata*—are all different varieties of the same species. They should be widely separated so they do not cross-pollinate. The foliage on the popcorn is pretty enough that it could be planted in the back of the flower border.

Corn is wind-pollinated and must be planted in blocks rather than in one long row. Without pollen blowing onto the tassels, the kernels will not form. Corn takes up a lot of space in a small garden for the amount of return, but if you like the wonderful taste of fresh-picked corn it will justify the space.
Harvest Time: Corn is harvested from August through September.
Height: 5 to 7 feet (1.5 to 2 m). Cobs will vary in length from a few inches (5 cm) in some of the ornamental corn varieties to 9 inches (23 cm) in some sweet corn.
Light and Soil: Corn will grow in average soil with a pH of 5.8 to 6.8. Corn is a heavy feeder so dig in some compost or manure, especially

poultry manure with its high phosphorus content. Corn needs full sun.
How to grow: Corn requires a warm soil—over 50°F (10°C)—for the seed to germinate. If it is sown too early the seeds will simply rot. Plant corn from mid-May through mid-June. Sow the seeds 1 to 2 inches (2.5 to 5 cm) deep and place 4 seeds to every foot (30 cm) or one seed every 3 inches (8 cm). When the corn is 5 inches (13 cm) tall, thin the plants so they are 6 to 10 inches (15 to 25 cm) apart. Leave 24 inches (60 cm) between the rows. Corn is shallow-rooted and care must be taken when weeding and hoeing not to injure the roots. Corn plants will grow roots above the soil as well as sending out smaller shoots. Do not remove them because they help to anchor the plant, but soil or mulch can be hilled up around the roots.

When the corn is seeded, fertilize the row with an all-purpose fertilizer like 6-8-6. When the seedlings are well established, side-dress with 20-20-20. When the ears are beginning to form, side-dress the plants with a high-nitrogen fertilizer such as 34-0-0.

There is usually no advantage to starting plants indoors because the direct-seeded crop will catch up to the transplanted one. Transplanting is a stress and it will slow the plants down. Clear plastic row covers may be set over the plants when they are seeded early. This could be done three weeks before it would be safe to plant them out, usually the first week of June on the coast. Remove the covers once the plants are ready to thin.

Seeds may be presprouted, which insures they have germinated. Soak the seeds in warm water for several hours, drain and place them in a zip lock bag with a small corner left open to allow air in. Place the bag on top of the refrigerator or some other warm spot until the root just begins to show—about one week.

Harvesting: Corn is ready to harvest when the husks turn a darker green and have filled out. The tassels (silks) will have turned brown. If a kernel is pierced and the juice is milky white, it is ripe. If the liquid is clear, it is not ripe enough to pick. Twist the cob off and, for supreme flavor, cook immediately. Old-timers say the water should already be boiling when the corn is picked. Newer varieties are sweeter, which gives them better keeping qualities. If corn is doughy or mealy it is overripe.

Popcorn and ornamental corns are left to dry on the plants. Remove them when the frosts come, or when the silks are dried up and the husks are bleached.

Storage: Fresh corn should be eaten immediately if possible; it can be stored in the husks for a week in the refrigerator. Corn can be frozen in the husks or the kernels can be removed and frozen.

Pests and Diseases: Earwigs, cutworms, slugs, seedcorn maggots and wireworms can attack corn. Several fungus diseases, including smut, may be a problem. See chapter six, Pests and Diseases, for further information on these pests.

Corn earworm, alias the tomato fruitworm, is not usually a problem for tomatoes but can cause a lot of damage to corn in the southern interior of British Columbia. The green, pink or brown, cutwormlike larva feeds on the silks and the top 20 to 30 percent of the kernels. The adult is a light golden brown moth that lays hundreds of eggs on the silks. There are several generations each summer. They do not overwinter in B.C. but are blown in on the winds, making them a sporadic pest. The only cultural remedy is to pick off the newly hatched larvae by hand.

Common smut and **head smut** attack corn. Common smut is more widespread and causes galls on the stems, leaves, ears and tassels. If the plant has common smut it will still have silks. The head smut galls replace the corn tassels and there will be no silks. Head smut is the most serious because it is systemic and it will move into all parts of the plant, including the roots. Through the roots it will get into the soil, where it will remain for several years. It was once thought that it could not survive this far north; though it is less common, it has been reported on the coast and in the interior of B.C. Cobs that are infected with smut are unappetizing to look at and are not edible, although common smut often infects only half the cob.

To help prevent smut, rotate the crops, grow resistant varieties and do not overfertilize. Remove infected plants and destroy them.

Varieties: In colder areas or for an early harvest, grow 'Northern Vee' or 'Polar Vee' because they have the shortest number of growing days. On the coast grow 'Golden Jubilee', 'Seneca Chief', 'Seneca Horizon' and 'Reward'. If you want to try one of the SE (sugar- enhanced) corns that have a higher sugar content for added tenderness, try 'Sugar Buns'. Different varieties of popcorn are fun to grow. 'White Cloud' is a good choice; 'Cutie Pops' and strawberry popcorn have 3-inch (8-cm) cobs that are very decorative. Ornamental corn varieties include calico or squaw corn.

CUCUMBER *Cucumis sativus*

Cucumbers are in the cucurbit family, which includes gourds, squash, pumpkins and melons. Cucumbers fit right in the middle for hardiness: the squashes are the hardiest and the melons the least hardy. Cucumbers are an ancient vegetable, native to India. Prehistoric travelers introduced it to the Far East and later the Spanish brought it to the Americas. When the explorers reached North America, the native Indians were already growing it.

There are some interesting cucumber varieties that are yellow and round in shape. Cucumbers grow well on the coast in most summers but they like it hot; if it is rainy, they will succumb to mildew.

The plants may be grown along the ground, up a trellis, or under cover if a parthenocarpic variety (one that does not need cross-pollination) is chosen, such as 'Euro-American'.

Harvest Time: July through September.

Height: The plants hug the ground unless they are trained onto a trellis.

Light and Soil: Cucumbers will grow in most soils, but a fairly rich loam will produce the best results. Raised beds will help to warm the soil. They need full sun and a pH between 6.0 and 8.0.

How to Grow: Cucumbers need a warm soil, above 60°F (15°C), to germinate and grow. They do poorly when the weather is cool and wet, so do not be in a rush to get the cucumbers out. Early June is the time to sow seed or set out transplants. Sow the seeds 1/2 to 1 inch (1 to 2.5 cm) deep. Plant several plants or seeds in a clump, or hill, allowing 3 feet (1 m) in each direction for the plants to sprawl. Hills have the advantage of heating up faster, but plants grown on a trellis will have fewer disease problems.

To grow cucumber on a trellis, leave 8 inches (20 cm) between the plants. Place the trellis on a 45-degree angle, supported by a couple of sturdy stakes, rather than straight up and down. The fruits as they grow will naturally hang down on the inside of the trellis. They are easy to harvest this way and they take up less garden space. The shady side could be planted with lettuce, which does better with a bit of shade during the heat of summer.

Before planting, dig compost into the soil and use an all-purpose fertilizer like 6-8-6 at planting or sowing time. Side-dress at about 4 weeks with a high-nitrogen fertilizer. Cucumbers are heavy feeders.

Transplants can be started four to six weeks before planting out, but start them in individual pots so the roots will not be disturbed when they are planted out.

Seeds can be presprouted by placing them on damp paper toweling, rolling it up and putting it in a plastic bag. Check the seeds each day and plant them when the root is just showing.

Cucumbers use a lot of water. Mulch the plants to keep the soil moisture even, but be sure the soil is warm before the mulch is added unless plastic is being used. It takes the sun longer to heat up the soil if it has to warm up an organic mulch first. Too much water causes stunting, but not enough water, uneven watering or excess nitrogen causes bitter or tasteless fruit. Soaker hoses work better than overhead watering to keep down disease problems. Wet leaves are more prone to fungus diseases.

Harvesting: The fruit is ready to harvest when the skin is shiny and bright. Once the fruit turns yellow, it is overripe. Keep the ripe cucumbers picked. If you miss a cucumber, pick it and discard it; the plant will stop producing if the overripe fruit is left on the vine. When harvesting, pick the fruit carefully so the vine is not injured.

Storage: Cucumbers will keep in the refrigerator for two weeks if wrapped in plastic. They are made into a variety of pickles.

Problems: Cucumber plants that do not produce fruit may not have been pollinated. To prevent this, grow more than one cucumber plant and do not cover the plants, as they are pollinated by insects. If the weather is cool and cloudy, pollination may be difficult, as the bees will not fly.

If the flowers fall off and do not set fruit, do not despair; the early flowers are always male and the female ones will come later, along with more male flowers. The female flower has a tiny cucumber below the flower.

Bitter fruit is usually a greenhouse problem and is due to heat that builds up under the glass. Outside cucumbers can also be affected if they are stressed from heat, lack of water or too much or too little fertilizer.

Pests and Disease: Cutworms, slugs, loopers and thrips, as well as several fungus diseases, including scab and powdery mildew, attack cucumbers. See chapter six, Pests and Diseases, for tips on how to deal with them.

Cucumbers are also subject to **scab**, which causes corky spots on the cucumbers that eventually become sunken and gray. The fungus overwinters on seed and crop residue. To prevent scab, rotate the cucurbit crops, practice good sanitation and buy resistant varieties.

Varieties: 'Marketmore' is a slicer cucumber that has resistance to scab and rarely becomes bitter. 'Bush Baby' is a pickling variety that grows on a compact, high-producing plant. 'Lemon Cucumber' is an old variety that is gaining popularity. It is a round, mild cucumber about the size of a lemon with a pale yellow skin.

EGGPLANT, or AUBERGINE *Solanum melongena*

Eggplant is not often grown on the coast. It really prefers hotter summers than we have here, but with a little help it can be grown. Eggplant is the Asian member of the tomato family, which originated in South America. It is an ancient vegetable that has been cultivated since prehistoric times and is the main ingredient in many Middle Eastern and Greek recipes.

Harvest Time: August to September.

Height: 10 to 20 inches (25 to 50 cm).

Light and Soil: The plants require fertile, well-drained soil. Grow them in full sun in a warm spot.

How to Grow: Start the seeds indoors the first week of April, eight weeks before they are set out in the beginning of June. Wait until the nights have warmed up to at least 45°F (8°C). Start the seeds on top of the refrigerator or other warm spot. The soil must be warm—75 to 80°F (24 to 26°C)—for the seeds to germinate.

Cover the garden soil with black plastic two weeks before the plants are set out. Be sure to harden the plants off before they are put into the garden. Set them 2 feet (60 cm) apart within the row and leave about the same distance between the rows. Cover the crop with Reemay for added warmth or take advantage of an empty cold frame to grow them in. Cloches can also be used to give them a head start, and they will do well if grown in a greenhouse. At planting time, give the plants some 6-8-6 and side-dress them with 6-8-6 when the plants start to set fruit.

Harvest Time: The fruits are ready to harvest when the skin is still shiny and they are 4 to 6 inches (10 to 15 cm) long, depending on the variety. The skin becomes dull when the fruit is overripe. If the fruit is harvested when it is not quite full-grown, it will encourage the plant to set more fruit. Check the plants carefully as the dark fruit is easily missed among the leaves. Some books claim the skin of the fruit is prickly, but this has not been the case in my experience; it may vary with different varieties.

Storage: Refrigerated, they will keep for two weeks.

Pests and Diseases: The plants are fairly problem free but are susceptible to the same diseases as tomatoes. Insect pests include flea beetles, aphids and cutworms. Refer to chapter six, Pests and Diseases, for further

information if any of these are a problem.
Varieties: 'Dusky' is a popular deep purple variety with good-sized fruit. 'Early Black Egg' and 'Black Bell' are rounder in shape than 'Dusky'. 'Baby Bell' produces miniature 2-inch (5-cm) fruits and is a good prospect for a 6-inch (15-cm) pot.

Hint: All eggplants will do very well in a container and they look attractive in the flower border. They have striking purple flowers that provoke many admiring comments.

I have been told that raw eggplants are poisonous, but after checking all my reference books, I could not find any mention of it. Nevertheless, eggplant never seems to be eaten raw.

CURLY ENDIVE and ESCAROLE *Chichorium endiva*

The deeply cut, curly form of this perennial plant is called endive, and the broader, smooth-leaf form is escarole. Endive does well on the coast, particularly if the summers are cool. It is likely native to the Mediterranean and has been eaten since the time of the Romans and early Greeks.

Endive and escarole are related to the blue-flowered chicory that grows wild in the province and are in the same family as lettuce. They are also good candidates for growing in a cold frame for early winter picking. They need the rain protection of the cold frame.

Height: Up to 12 inches (30 cm).

Harvest Time: The plants are harvested in the late spring. Depending on the summer, they might be harvested through to the fall.

Light and Soil: Endive does well in any reasonably fertile soil. It does not mind the acid soils of the coast and will grow in a range of pH 5.0 to 6.8. It will tolerate some shade but does well in full sun as long as the season isn't too hot.

How to Grow: The plants are quite heavy feeders and some 6-8-6 should be sprinkled along the row when the seeds are sown. Once the plants are established, side-dress them with more fertilizer. Sow the seeds 1/2 inch (1 cm) deep and space the plants 12 to 18 inches (30 to 45 cm) apart. Plant them in multiple rows with the same spacing between rows as within the row. Water well and mulch in the summer to conserve moisture. The seeds can be sown in mid-April for a late spring harvest and again in mid-July for fall harvest. For a fall crop, sow seeds in the cold frame at the end of August.

Blanching the plants three to five weeks before they are to be harvested makes for tender, tasty leaves. To blanch, tie the leaves together.

Harvesting: The plants can be harvested leaf by leaf or the whole plant can be cut off. A light frost sweetens the plants.
Storage: Leaves will keep a week in the refrigerator, wrapped in plastic.
Problems: Some bitterness is natural; blanching and frost sweeten the plant. Bolting can occur if it is too cold when the plants are young or if they are under stress.
Pests and Diseases: The plants are fairly problem free.
Varieties: 'President' is a frilly, very dark green endive that is quite frost hardy. 'Full Heart Batavian' is a smooth, dark green escarole with creamy center leaves; it tolerates low temperatures.

JERUSALEM ARTICHOKE, SUN CHOKE, GIRASOLE *Helianthus tuberosus*

The name Jerusalem artichoke is a bit of a misnomer. The plant has nothing to do with the Middle East, and although it is a member of the sunflower family, the same as the globe artichoke, they are distinctly different and only distantly related. The Jerusalem artichoke has yellow, daisylike flowers and the globe artichoke has a purple, thistlelike flower head. It is suspected that Jerusalem is a corruption of girasole, which means turn to the sun. Both sunflowers (*Helianthus annuus*) and Jerusalem artichokes are native to North America.

The Jerusalem artichoke was used for food by some Indian tribes, but in many areas it is considered a weed. It is almost impossible to get rid of all the tubers once the plant is grown in an area. If the tubers are left unharvested, the patch will increase yearly. The plant is hardy and will grow without too much care or attention. It is grown for its club-shaped underground stem, called a tuber, which resembles the fresh ginger root that you can buy at the market. The crispy, textured tubers can be baked, boiled, used in stews or eaten raw. Cook them any way you would a potato, but do not overcook them. The flavor is subtle and nutty and they are crunchy when eaten raw. The Jerusalem artichoke is often marketed as sunchoke in the grocery stores.

For the garden, many catalogues and nurseries carry Jerusalem tubers. Once you have a couple of tubers you are set for life. When you harvest them, save enough to replant in the spring for next year's crop.
Harvest Time: Jerusalem artichokes are harvested throughout the winter.
Height: 6 feet (2 m).
Light and Soil: Plant the tubers in a sunny, well-drained area, preferably one that is out of the way, as the plants are tall. Jerusalem artichokes will

grow in most soils, but they are easier to harvest if the soil is easy to dig.
How to Grow: Plant the tubers in the early spring, 4 to 6 inches (10 to 15 cm) deep and 18 to 24 inches (45 to 60 cm) apart. Established beds should be dug up in the early spring and the unharvested tubers replanted for the new season. Dig the bed each spring; the plants, if left, will form a dense mat of tubers and can become an impossible, weedy patch. When the bed is replanted, rake in some 6-8-6 fertilizer. Keep the plants watered during dry spells.
Harvesting: The tubers are harvested as needed from fall onwards. The tubers keep best in the ground rather than digging and storing them, as long as the ground does not freeze hard and is well drained.
Storage: Store the tubers in a plastic bag in the refrigerator for up to two weeks. For longer storage, layer them in sand in a dry, cool, above-freezing place.
Pests and Diseases: They are usually free of pests and diseases except for an occasional infestation of wireworms.
Varieties: They are usually sold as unnamed varieties, in packages of 8 to 10 tubers. The tubers are available in nurseries or from catalogues, such as Dominion Seed House. Try to share a package, as one package will likely be too many for one family. Buy the larger, domestic, cultivated tubers and do not use the smaller wild tubers. Tubers purchased from markets can also be planted.
Hint: Jerusalem artichokes are a source of inulin, which is a safe carbohydrate for diabetics, and is used in making diabetic breads.

KALE *Brassica oleracea*

Kale crops are one of the best values for the space used in a vegetable garden. On the coast, the plants are harvested leaf by leaf through the summer and well into the winter. The stems are delicious steamed or stir-fried, and the tender leaves are good in salads. The leaves are smooth or curled and may also be steamed. Frosts will sweeten the leaves; in the summer they can be put in a plastic bag and refrigerated for a few days to sweeten them.

Kale has been under cultivation for thousands of years and has been in North America since the first settlers arrived. Many thousands of years ago cabbage would have resembled the present-day kale. There is also an edible, ornamental kale that is treated like the flowering cabbage. The colorful leaves of both the ornamental and vegetable kale make attractive garnishes.

Harvest Time: Kale is harvested from July through to the next spring depending on the winter.
Height: Up to 3 feet (90 cm).
Light and Soil: The soil should be loamy, with compost dug in and a pH of between 6.0 and 6.8. Plant kale in full sun for best results, although it will grow in light shade. Winter picking and good drainage for fall rains should be considered when the site is chosen.
How to Grow: Kale can be sown direct or placed out as transplants. It grows best when the weather is cool. Put some transplants out in May and seed some of the hardier varieties in June or July for later harvesting. Plant the seeds 1/2 inch (1 cm) deep and thin to 12 inches (30 cm). The rows should be 18 inches (45 cm) apart. If the weather is hot, a light mulch will help the seeds germinate. The overwintering plants will not grow during the winter, but will add more growth as the weather warms in the spring. Side-dress when the new growth starts in the spring. Even in severe winters, kale and spinach will survive.
Harvesting: Remove the bottom leaves rather than taking the whole head. They will come off with a twist near the stem. The flavor is enhanced after a frost. Be careful to not remove the terminal end, which is the growing tip of the plant.
Storage: Kale is best eaten as it is harvested. It can be stored a few days in plastic in the refrigerator, but the leaves become bitter if they are left for too long.
Pests and Diseases: Kale is subject to the same pests and diseases as the other brassicas: various fungus diseases, aphids, cutworms, cabbage looper, flea beetle, wireworms and the ever-present imported cabbage-worm. Refer to chapter six, Pests and Diseases, for tips on controlling these problems.
Varieties: 'Green Curled Scotch' has extremely curly leaves with a hint of yellow in the green. 'Siberian' and 'Winterbor' F1 are both good choices for the coast.

KOHLRABI *Brassica oleracea*

Kohlrabi is an odd-looking vegetable, with leaf stalks sticking out all around the swollen stem. Kohlrabi can be pale green or purple with light green flesh and has a delicate flavor when it is picked young. The flavor is a cross between a turnip and a cabbage, which its name reflects. In German, *kohl* means cabbage and *rabi* means turnip. Its history is uncertain, but it was grown in Italian gardens in the 16th century.

Kohlrabi is great in a stir-fry or served raw cut into sticks. The golfball-sized kohlrabi can be eaten skin and all, but the larger ones are tough-skinned and must be peeled.

Harvest Time: Kohlrabi is harvested in June and July or as a fall crop in October and November.

Height: 12 to 15 inches (30 to 45 cm).

Light and Soil: The soil should be well prepared with added organic matter and have a pH of 6.0 to 7.0. Keep the plants well watered to get them growing quickly and do not let the soil dry out. Plant them in full sun or light shade.

How to Grow: Kohlrabi can be grown from transplants but it does very well from seed. Sow in small amounts, successively from April through to mid-June. An all-purpose fertilizer like 6-8-6 should be used at sowing. The plants do not do well in hot weather and are tastier if they mature when the weather is cool—usually not a problem on the coast. Sow 1/2 inch (1 cm) deep and thin the plants to 12 inches (30 cm) apart. The tender thinnings can be cooked leaf and all.

A second sowing may be done the end of July through August for fall harvesting. Hoe carefully around the plants because they have a shallow root system.

Harvesting: The plants are ready to eat when the swollen part of the stem is 2 inches (5 cm) across. When they are larger, they become woody and stronger in flavor. The fall crop may be harvested when it is slightly larger in size; the cooler weather seems to keep them from getting quite so tough. To harvest, pull up the whole plant and cut off the leaves. Peel off the outer layer before eating.

Storage: Kohlrabi keeps a couple of weeks in the refrigerator wrapped in plastic. It can also be frozen.

Problems: Hollow cavities inside the kohlrabi may indicate a boron deficiency or may mean the plant is overmature. Manures, compost and fertilizers that contain micronutrients will contain boron.

Pests and Diseases: They are fairly pest free but are susceptible to the same diseases as other cole crops; clubroot, aphids, loopers, cutworms and the imported cabbageworm can all be a problem occasionally. Refer to chapter six, Pests and Diseases, for further information on these pests.

Varieties: 'Early White Vienna' and 'Early Purple Vienna' are two standard varieties that perform well. Bright, purple-skinned 'Rapid' and the light green 'Winner' F1 both hold up well in the garden and do not become woody or bolt for quite a while after they reach maturity.

LEEKS *Allium ampeloprasum*

A relative of the onion, leeks have a long growing season and are very hardy. Their mild flavor is enhanced by frost and they can be harvested throughout the winter. They are a cool-season vegetable that does well on the coast. Unless they are picked very young, for salads, leeks are cooked.

Leeks have a long history, both as a vegetable and a medicinal plant. The Welsh wore them into battle and to this day they are worn on St. David's Day to commemorate the Welsh victory over the Saxons.

Harvest Time: Late September to April.

Height: 18 to 24 inches (45 to 60 cm).

Light and Soil: Plant leeks in fertile, well-drained soil that has had lots of compost dug into it. Soil should have a pH of 6.0 to 7.5. Plant in full sun or in light shade.

How to Grow: Early varieties should be started indoors in March for planting out in May. Overwintering varieties can be started in March as well or direct-seeded in May. Top-dress with an all-purpose fertilizer like 6-8-6 when the leeks are sown or transplanted. Leeks are heavy feeders with a long growing period of up to 150 days, so they will need to be side-dressed throughout the season. Set the transplants deep and either hill the plants up as they grow or start them off in an 8-inch-deep (20-cm) trench and gradually fill in the soil as the leeks grow. This will blanch the stems. Sow seeds 1/2 inch (5 cm) deep and thin to 4 inches (10 cm) apart in the row. The rows should be 18 inches (45 cm) apart. Hand-weed because the roots are very shallow. Mulching will help to conserve moisture as well as blanch the stems.

Harvesting: When the leeks are 1 inch (2.5 cm) or more in diameter, they may be picked. Leeks that are left longer will grow to 2 or 3 inches (5 or 8 cm). Pull the plants and cut off the roots and the upper portion of the leaves. To clean leeks before cooking, discard the outer leaves and soak the leek for awhile, then hold it under running water to remove all the soil.

Storage: If possible, harvest leeks as they are needed. On the coast they will keep well in the garden most years. They can be stored upright in moist sand at 32°F (0°C) if the area is too cold to leave them out over the winter. They keep well for about three weeks, wrapped in plastic, in the refrigerator.

Problems: Bolting, which happens infrequently, is usually caused by fluctuating temperatures and moisture. Plants may bolt if they are too large when transplanted; they should be no larger than the thickness of a pencil.

Pests and Diseases: Leeks are very pest and disease free. Any problems they might have are the same as the rest of the onion family.
Varieties: 'Durabel' is a mild-flavored, winter-hardy leek that will survive most winters on the coast. 'Splendid' is a fast-growing leek that will be ready to harvest in the fall. It is not as hardy as 'Durabel'.

LETTUCE *Lactuca sativa*

Lettuce is a crop that does well with our cooler West Coast weather. We can have lettuce most of the year if some of the hardy varieties are overwintered in a cold frame. A member of the Compositae, the daisy family, it is a very old vegetable that was written about by the Greeks in the fifth century B.C.
Harvest Time: Most of the year.
Height: 6 to 12 inches (15 to 30 cm).
Light and Soil: Lettuce does best in well-drained, rich, friable soil that has been amended with manure. It is a crop that requires lots of nitrogen. The soil should have a pH of 5.8 to 6.8. Summer crops will grow in light shade, but at other times of the year lettuce needs full sun.
How to Grow: Start sowing in small amounts in April and continue through to mid-August for the cold-hardy varieties, such as 'Winter Density'. By using a cold frame, you can get a head start on the season, sowing lettuce in March. Sow the seeds 1/2 inch (1 cm) deep and cover them lightly with soil. Lettuce seeds need some light to germinate. Thin the seedlings to 8 to 12 inches (20 to 30 cm) apart, depending on the type of lettuce. The rows can be 15 inches (38 cm) apart. If the rows are not thinned enough, there may be disease problems, such as fungus rots, and the lettuce will not develop properly. Thinnings may be transplanted or eaten. Lettuce must be watered well or its growth will be slowed and it will become bitter. In the warmer weather lettuce will bolt. There are varieties that are resistant to bolting, but lettuce does not generally hold well after it reaches maturity.

Lettuce is a good crop to interplant between crops that take longer to mature, such as the cole crops.
Harvesting: Except for head lettuce, individual leaves can be harvested. This is a boon for gardeners with small space and small families. There is a limit to how long you can pick the lettuce this way, but it does extend the harvest. When harvesting whole heads, pull the plant out of the ground, roots and all. If the roots are washed off and left on the heads, it will prolong storage life.

Storage: Lettuce will keep for a week, wrapped in plastic in the refrigerator. Wrap the roots in a wet paper towel to increase storage life.
Problems: If the soil is too warm, the lettuce seed will not break its dormancy. This is usually not a problem on the coast. Watering the soil will cool it and a layer of sifted compost over the seeds will also help.
Pests and Diseases: There are several fungus rot diseases that attack lettuce during wet seasons. Crop rotation and air circulation will help to prevent them. Pull and destroy all diseased plants.

Slugs, cutworms, earwigs, wireworms and lettuce aphids may attack the crop. For tips on how to deal with these pests, see chapter six, Pests and Diseases.
Varieties: 'Red Sails' is a tender lettuce that is pretty enough to grow in the flower border. 'Buttercrunch' is a small open lettuce that is often in the grocery stores during the winter. It is easy to grow in the garden and takes the summer heat well. 'Valmaine' is a cos or romaine type—a tall, football-shaped lettuce. 'Slo Bolt' is a variety bred from 'Grand Rapid' type lettuce. It forms a very attractive rosette of leaves and is a good choice for growing in the cold frame in the early spring or fall. 'Winter Density', a romaine type, does very well on the coast and withstands some frost.

MUSKMELON or CANTALOUPE *Cucumis melo*

Melons do very well on the coast, especially considering they are a tropical plant. At the University of British Columbia they have done better than expected, especially during summers when the weather has been less than ideal.

It is suspected that melons are native to India; their early history is unknown, but they have been under cultivation for at least 4,000 years. The true cantaloupe is a melon grown in Asia but cantaloupe has become a generic name for several different muskmelons, such as honeydew, winter melons and casaba melons.
Harvest Time: Late August to September.
Height: 6 inches (15 cm), on a sprawling vine.
Light and Soil: Melons need rich, well-drained soil treated with an all-purpose fertilizer like 6-8-6. Cover the area with black plastic several weeks before setting out the transplants. Raised beds are an advantage, as the soil will be warmer. Plant in full sun.
How to Grow: Do not sow seeds directly; start transplants indoors in April in individual pots. Set them in a cold frame the last week of May, where they will stay until they are planted in the garden at the end of the

first week of June. Make cross-slits in the plastic, and set the plants into the ground 3 feet (1 m) apart. Using a pitchfork, make small holes in the plastic for water to drain through. Water the plants deeply.

The male flowers will appear first, and the female flowers with the small bulb at the base will follow, along with more male flowers. If the plants have been covered with Reemay for extra protection, it must be removed once the plants begin to flower, so that bees can pollinate the flowers.

Harvesting: Allow the fruit to ripen on the vine. Melons are ripe when they separate easily from the stem. Probably the easiest test of ripeness is to use your nose—ripe melons have a distinctive smell. The outer skin will have changed to a lighter color.

Storage: Melons will only keep a few days after they ripen.

Pests and Diseases: Cool, wet weather will cause several fungus diseases, including powdery mildew, which, if heavy, can stop production. The cure is hot, dry weather. Plant resistant varieties and give them the warmest spot in the garden.

There are several insect pests that could attack the crop, such as loopers and cutworms, but melons are generally fairly free of pests. For further information see chapter six, Pests and Diseases.

Varieties: 'Canada Gem' has a tasty, deep orange flesh and it is tolerant of powdery mildew. 'Earlygold' F1 and 'Earlidew' F1 are two early-ripening varieties. 'Sakata's Resistant Joy' F1 is a disease-tolerant variety that does well on the coast when the weather is damp and cool.

ONION *Allium cepa*

The onion is another ancient vegetable that was used medicinally as well as for food. It was used in sacred rites in many early cultures, from Egypt to the Orient. Its origin is unknown but it likely came from the Mediterranean or Asia Minor.

Onions are perennials that we grow as annuals. They are grown from onion sets or from seed. Onion does well when started outside in our cool springs. It is a universal vegetable that can grow almost anywhere in the world and there are few homes that haven't used it as a flavoring or a vegetable.

There are lovely, pink, white, purple and mauve ornamental onions that are grown in flower gardens.

Harvest Time: Onions are harvested from summer through to winter.

Height: Up to 18 inches (45 cm).

Light and Soil: Onions need fertile, moist soil that has had compost and peat dug into it. Bunching onions will tolerate some shade, but most onions need to be grown in the sun.

How to Grow: Onion sets are dormant onions that are sold in grocery and department stores and garden centers. They are easy to plant. Just place them so the tip is at the soil surface, about 4 inches (10 cm) apart.

It is easy and cheaper to start plants from seed. Start the larger, sweeter onions inside from seed in February. Sow seeds outside from April through May. Place the seeds 1/2 inch (1 cm) deep, leaving one foot (30 cm) between rows. To make better use of space, plant onions in a band of four rows across. Gradually thin the bulbs to 3 inches (8 cm) apart. If every second onion is removed each time you thin, there will be a continuous supply of green onions over the summer. The ones that are finally left can be harvested at maturity. Keep the rows weed free; onions have very small root systems and they cannot compete with the weeds.

Band the onions with a complete fertilizer like 6-8-6 by sprinkling the fertilizer along the row. Side-dress the rows with 6-8-6 after the plants are established. Keep the fertilizer close to the plants, as the roots only extend for be about 4 to 6 inches (10 to 15 cm) on either side of the plant. If an onion develops a thick stem, pull it and use it, as it will not store well.

Onions like 'Sweet Winter' can be seeded in late August for a spring crop. Fertilize only lightly; too much nitrogen will result in softer growth that reduces winter hardiness. Side-dress in the late winter when the plants are thinned.

Harvesting: Use the thinnings for salads. Mature onions are ready to harvest when the tips of the leaves turn brown and the leaves begin to fall over. Any leaves that have not fallen over should be knocked down when the tips brown. This helps the plants harden off so they will keep better. If possible, let the soil dry out. After a week, carefully dig the onions and leave them to dry in the sun for two to three days, depending on the weather. Protect them from dew at night. If the weather is wet, dry them in a carport or a basement.

Storage: Cooking onions will keep most of the winter in a dry, frost-free place, with temperatures of 55 to 65°F (12 to 17°C). The onions can be braided or stored in net bags or old nylon stockings. Suspending the bags allows air to circulate and increases the storage life. Depending on the variety, sweet onions will keep for a month or so.

Pests and Diseases: Onions in the home garden seem to be fairly problem free, but they are susceptible to fungus and smut diseases. Crop rotation, sanitation and plenty of air circulation will help to make a problem-free crop.

Onion maggots only attack onions and are a problem throughout B.C. They feed on the root, causing the bulb to be distorted or killing the plant. Use Reemay to protect the plants.

Onion thrips are more of a problem in the interior of the province but they may also appear in gardens on the coast. Thrips can also attack cucurbits, beans, tomatoes and cole crops. The leaves take on a silvery look as the insect sucks the plant juice. Eventually they may die and the yield will be poor. The insect has at least three generations and it overwinters on weeds and garden refuse. Sanitation and weed control will help to prevent thrips.

Varieties: There are some unusual onions that are passed from friend to friend, such as the Egyptian onion and an onion that has its bulbs at the tip of the stem. Occasionally they may be available in catalogues. 'Early Yellow Sweet' and 'White Sweet Spanish' are two sweet onions that are poor keepers but very tasty. 'White Lisbon' and 'Southport White Globe' are two well-known early onion varieties that produce bunching onions for fresh use. For storage grow 'Simcoe' F1, a yellow-skinned onion, and 'Bennies Red'. Both do well on the coast. 'Sweet Winter' and 'Kurenai Red' F1 are both varieties that are seeded in August and harvested the following June.

PARSNIP *Pastinaca sativa*

Parsnips are a biennial that would bloom in the second season, if allowed to, but they are always harvested in the first year. They are a starchy vegetable that tastes better after there has been a frost or two because the starch turns to sugar. Parsnips take up a fair amount of space but are a fairly care-free crop. They look like a sturdy, whitish carrot and they do belong to the same family.

Parsnips likely originated in the Mediterranean area, where they were gathered in the wild. By the 1500s they were commonly grown in Europe.

Harvest Time: Late fall and throughout the winter.

Height: 2 feet (60 cm).

Light and Soil: The soil should be deep; the roots, depending on the variety, can be 12 inches (30 cm) long. Use compost to increase the water retention in the soil. Do not add manure, as it will result in hairy, forked roots. The seeds should be sown on well-drained soil. Parsnips do best in full sun but will tolerate light shade. Raised beds will improve the drainage, an advantage since the roots will be in the ground over winter. Parsnips need soil with a pH of 6.0 or higher.

How to Grow: Parsnips need a long growing season. Sow the seeds from the end of April through to June. If radishes are sown with the parsnips, they will germinate faster and help the parsnips break through the soil. If parsnips are seeded alone, keep the soil moist and prevent it from crusting over. Parsnip seeds do not keep well, so buy fresh ones each year. Sow the seeds 1/2 inch (1 cm) deep and 1/2 inch (1 cm) apart. Thin seedlings to 4 inches (10 cm) apart, depending on the variety. Parsnip seeds have a low germination rate and it is better to sow the seeds 1/2 inch (1 cm) apart and thin the seedlings, rather than having a lot of misses in the row. An alternative method is to plant 3 seeds at 4- inch (10-cm) intervals. Once they have their first set of true leaves, remove all but the strongest seedling.

Harvesting: Wait until after the first frost to harvest the roots. They improve with frost and can benefit from several frosts. Harvest them as needed over the winter.

Storage: Leave parsnips in the ground. In areas where the ground freezes, dig the roots after the first light frost and store them in sand in a cold storage room.

Pests and Diseases: Parsnips are generally fairly free of problems, but they may be troubled with the carrot rust fly and aphids. Cover the plants with Reemay at seeding. Carrot rust fly is covered in the Carrots entry.

Canker can be a problem in wet seasons. It can cause leaf spots and root rot, usually at an injury site which is often caused by the rust fly. Later, bacterial infections may move in.

Varieties: There are only a few parsnip varieties available but 'Harris Model' is an excellent variety with a very smooth, white root.

PEAS *Pisum sativum*

Peas are grown for their seeds and often for their edible pod. Garden peas and edible pod peas do well in our moist cool climate. They take up a lot of room but few gardeners can resist the taste of fresh-picked peas. They are delicious cooked, but it is sometimes hard to get out of the garden before eating them. One year at the UBC Botanical Garden, we sent some peas to the extended care hospital on campus. The residents enjoyed shelling the peas, which reminded them of happy times.

Peas have been grown for centuries and seed was recovered from the tombs at Thebes. Henry Daniels, a 14th-century herbalist, lists both white and green peas growing in Normandy. The original peas were not as tender and sweet as today's peas and were grown as field peas for cattle. The tender-podded peas we grow today have only arrived on the market in the last ten years. Regular garden peas are constantly being improved: new varieties are introduced each year.

Harvest Time: Peas are harvested from June through July.

Height: 1 to 7 feet (.3 to 2m).

Light and Soil: Plant peas in a rich, well-drained soil that is not too high in nitrogen. Peas will tolerate light shade if necessary, but they will do better in full sun. They grow best at pH 6.0 to 6.5.

How to Grow: Plant peas from the middle of March through the end of June. If the seeds are planted too early and the soil is very wet, the seeds will rot and germination will be spotty. Sow the seeds 1 inch (2.5 cm) deep and 1 inch (2.5 cm) apart. Plant double or single rows, with 15 inches (38 cm) between the rows. Peas germinate best when the weather is cool, from 40 to 60°F (5 to 15°C). They do not need to be thinned. Plant bush peas in succession until May.

If the garden is new, use an innoculant for peas. The use of innoculents is discussed in the Beans entry. Peas need some nitrogen when the seeds are sown. Use 6-8-6 to get them going, and do not fertilize them again.

Tall varieties need support, and even the bush peas benefit from stakes or twiggy branches. The sugar snap peas need more than just netting; the plants are heavy and pull away from the netting.

Harvesting: Peas are ready for picking when the pods are full but there is still space between the peas. Keep the plants picked and remove any overripe pods that were missed. If the ripe pods are not removed, the plants will stop producing—the life cycle of an annual ends when it produces ripe seed. Bush peas tend to be ready all at once, while the tall and edible-pod peas have a longer season.

Storage: Eat peas fresh off the vine if possible. They also freeze well. They will keep in the refrigerator, wrapped in plastic, for several days.

Pests and Diseases: Peas are susceptible to several fungus diseases. Rotate the crop and practice good sanitation. Insects that may be a problem are cabbage loopers, aphids, weevils, slugs and wireworms. See chapter six, Pests and Diseases, for controls of these pests.

Varieties: 'Tall Telephone' for staking and 'Improved Laxtons Progress', a dwarf vine, are two older varieties of shelling peas that are worth growing. 'Sugar Snap' and 'Sugar Ann' are my favorite snap peas with edible pods. 'Sugar Snaps' are very difficult to hold on netting because the weight of the vines will pull them over. Use chicken wire on sturdy posts to hold the vines. 'Sugar Ann' is low-growing and should not be picked until the pods are full; the sugar content is higher then and they will be sweeter. 'Sugar Snap' has already been replaced in some catalogues by improved varieties that are stringless and have more compact vines, but I suspect it will always have its fans (the strings pull off easily). 'Rembrandt' is a delicious snow pea to add to the stir-fry. It is very sweet, especially if the pods are allowed to mature a little. One pea variety, 'Novella', is a mass of curly tendrils which help to hold the vines up with little staking. Unfortunately the pods are difficult to pick because of all the tendrils. But new varieties are always fun to try and what may not suit one gardener may be the answer for another.

PEPPERS *Capsicum annuum*

Peppers are another heat-loving crop that does amazingly well on the West Coast although they are native to tropical South and Central America. Peppers were grown by the Aztecs and other early civilizations. It was Christopher Columbus who took peppers back to Europe—because they were hot they were called pepper, after the spice. Peppers are closely related to tomatoes, eggplants and potatoes, which are all native to the tropical areas of the Americas.

Peppers are now grown in every country around the world. There are hundreds of different varieties in various shapes and sizes and they can be mild to fiery hot. Peppers add the fire to Mexican, Oriental and Indian cuisine. The bell or sweet peppers have recently become available in a rainbow of colors—purple, green, yellow—and at maturity most will turn red. The hot peppers are affected by weather and will be much hotter when they are grown in a hot, dry climate than they will be on the coast, where it is cool and damp.

Ornamental peppers, or "capsicum," are very attractive plants for the flower border or containers. Some, but not all, have edible fruits.

Harvest Time: August to September.

Height: 1 to 2 feet (30 to 60 cm).

Light and Soil: Peppers do best in a light, loamy soil that is well drained. Peppers need full sun.

How to grow: Peppers have a long growing season and they must be started indoors by March 1 at the latest. They need warm soil to germinate—27 to 29°C (80 to 85°F). The plants take up a lot of space unless you have a warm greenhouse or other warm place for them. They will need a temperature of 66 to 78°F (18 to 24°C) during the day and 62 to 66°F (16 to 18°C) at night.

Peppers must not be put outside until the night temperature is greater than 55°F (13°C), usually some time in June. This is very important; if they are subject to cold they will not set fruit and any fruit that has already set may drop. To do well, peppers must have a hot spot in the garden and the soil should be covered with black plastic a week before they are planted out. They are a good candidate for raised beds or tubs. If the nights are cool after the peppers have been planted out, put a cloche over the plants as necessary. Reemay will also raise the temperature (it will only raise it a few degrees but it may be sufficient to protect the plants). Peppers should be planted 12 to 15 inches (30 to 38 cm) apart.

In the last week of August, remove any flowers, as they will not have time to develop into fruit. Keep the plants evenly watered during the growing season. Hot and sweet peppers are given the same care, although hot peppers need more heat than sweet peppers. On the coast they will do better in years when the summers are warmer.

Harvesting: Pick the fruit when it has sized up and the flesh looks shiny. Green peppers will gradually turn red in color if they are left on the plant and they will be sweeter in flavor. Hot peppers can be harvested plant and all. Hang the plant in a warm spot and the peppers will dry and shrivel on the plant. When harvesting peppers, use pruners to snip off the fruit or gently twist them off the plant.

Storage: Peppers will keep at least one week in the refrigerator. They can be frozen or used in pickles.

Pests and Diseases: In the home garden, peppers are relatively free of disease, but may be susceptible to blossom end rot and virus diseases. Insect pests are cutworms, flea beetles and aphids. See chapter six, Pests and Diseases, if you have those problems.

Varieties: 'Purple Bell', 'Golden Bell' and 'Earlycal Wonder' are three bell-type peppers to try; 'Golden Bell' does well in cooler gardens and 'Earlycal Wonder', a green pepper, turns a deep wine red as it matures. Some of the smaller-fruited sweet peppers are worth growing. Some are long and thinner than the bell peppers. 'Gypsy' F1, a pale yellow pepper, produces heavily. For hot peppers, try 'Anaheim', a milder hot pepper, 'Long Thick Red', a long red fruit that is very hot and 'Early Jalapeno', which tolerates cooler conditions.

Hint: String the dried hot peppers and tie the top with a raffia bow for an attractive and edible kitchen decoration. Use a needle and a sturdy linen thread to string the peppers or twist a string around the stem of each pepper. Start at the bottom and work your way up. Large, dried red peppers are very attractive as decorations on a Christmas tree.

POTATOES *Solanum tuberosum*

Potatoes are considered one of the most humble of vegetables, but until you have grown your own you haven't really experienced the true taste of this vegetable. The plants take up a lot of room, but even a few plants are worth it when you cook those tiny new potatoes.

Potatoes are native to South America and were introduced to Europe by Christopher Columbus in the 16th century. There is a lot of history bound up in the potato; the great Irish famine of 1846-1847 was a result of the failure of the potato crop. Many people died and as a direct result of the famine many Irish emigrated to North America. Looking back, we can pinpoint the reasons for that crop failure. The temperature and humidity was right for potato blight and the crop had no resistance. All the potatoes were from the same genetic stock, crops were not rotated and culls that provided the innoculum were left in piles by the fields.

Some people are startled to find a fruit that resembles a tomato growing on their potato plant. Potatoes and tomatoes are members of the same family so it is not surprising that their fruits look alike, although the fruit of the potato is not edible. Their flowers also reveal the similarity. The two plants are so closely related that you can graft a tomato onto a potato—the tomato growing on top and the potatoes in the ground. Occasionally these plants are offered for sale as a novelty.

There are three basic types of potatoes: the mealy-textured ones such as the russets, which are used for baking; the moister white potatoes, such as 'Kennebec', which are boiled and fried; and the red-skinned potatoes for boiling, such as the well-known 'Red Pontiac'. There are many older and unusual varieties that are sometimes available, such as 'Banana' which comes from Russia. It has shown disease resistance and has a good flavor.

Harvest Time: June through October.

Height: 2 feet (60 cm).

Light and Soil: Potatoes will grow in most soils, but they will do best in a deep, well-drained soil that has had compost and well-rotted manure added to it. The soil should have a pH of 4.8 to 5.6. This will help prevent and control scab disease. Plant potatoes in full sun.

How to Grow: Although potatoes are not usually propagated from seed, the potatoes that are sold to grow the crop are referred to as "seed." Seed potatoes are available from some catalogues and from garden centers, and grocery and department stores in the spring. The seed potatoes sold in British Columbia are certified virus free. You can't use the potatoes you buy to eat, because they are treated with chemicals to prevent them from sprouting.

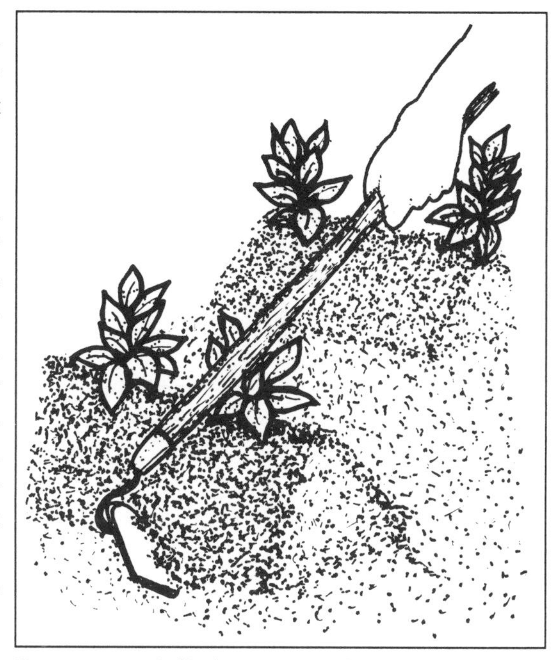

Potatoes are hilled to protect developing tubers from the sun.

About two weeks before the potatoes are to be planted out, place them in a flat or on a tray in a light, airy, warm room at about 70°F (20°C). Do not leave them in the sun. The potatoes will start to produce shoots. Just before planting, cut the potatoes into pieces, each piece containing several eyes or shoots. If the potatoes are very small, the size of a walnut, plant them whole. Treat the sprouted potatoes with care or the shoots will be knocked off.

Use small whole potatoes if you can, as there is less chance of disease entering when there is no open cut. These small seed potatoes are seen more frequently now and they are traditionally used in Europe.

Early potatoes are planted mid-March, providing the soil is well drained, through until April. Later potatoes may be planted up to mid-June. Potatoes need about a 3-month growing period.

Dig a trench about 6 inches (15 cm) deep. Place the seed potato in the trench with the eyes uppermost. Space them 12 inches (30 cm) apart with 15 inches (38 cm) between the rows. Cover the pieces with several inches of soil. If the soil is rich with well-rotted manure, no further fertilizer may be needed. If you are applying fertilizer, use an all-purpose one like 6-8-6. Potatoes will produce more leaves than tubers if they have too much nitrogen.

As they grow, mound up more soil or straw around the plants. The advantage of straw is the tubers stay cleaner. Tubers will form along the buried stem. It is important to keep the soil or straw mounded, so the developing tubers are not exposed to the sun, which turns the exposed area green and makes it toxic. Always discard any green tubers.

Once the tubers have started to form, do not allow the plants to dry out.

Harvesting: Once the flowers appear, the early potatoes are usually ready to harvest. Uncover a bit of the plant or wiggle your hand down and check on the size of the tubers. If the potatoes are an inch (2.5 cm) in diameter, they are ready to harvest. The new potatoes can be removed without disturbing the plant, which allows the rest to grow before they are harvested. I dig out enough for a meal each day. The main crop is harvested as the tops die back in the late summer through fall. If possible, allow the soil to dry out before lifting the tubers out. Spread them out and let them dry off completely before storing.

Storage: Early varieties must be used as soon as they are harvested. Late varieties will keep for four to nine months. Store only blemish-free tubers. Keep them in a frost-free place, at a temperature of 35°F (3°C), and cover them with a sheet of black plastic to keep out the light.

Pests and Diseases: Insects that commonly attack potato crops are wireworms, aphids and beetles, such as flea beetles and June beetles. Several bacterial diseases can attack potatoes, as well as viruses, rots, and fungus diseases, such as early and late potato blight, which also infect tomatoes. For tips on how to deal with these problems, refer to chapter six, Pests and Diseases. Tomato blight is dealt with in the Tomato entry.

Scab is a soil-borne fungus disease that causes rough, corky growths on the potato skin. To control the disease, do not lime and use resistant varieties, such as the russets.

For a healthy potato crop, always buy certified stock, rotate the crop, remove weeds, control aphids, do not overfertilize, lime or use fresh manure, and remove all debris after harvest—especially potatoes that are damaged or diseased.

Varieties: 'Warba' is an early variety that is an old standard and well worth growing in the home garden. 'Yukon Gold' has yellow flesh and even though it is an early variety it can be stored. 'Norland', 'Kennebec' and 'Yukon Gold' are midseason varieties. For a late-maturing crop, try 'Russet Burbank', a netted gem variety released in 1874, which is an excellent storage and baking potato.

RADISH *Raphanus sativus*

Radish is a cool-weather annual. It grows quickly and can be sown between slower-growing vegetables like peas, cabbages and cauliflower. The radishes will be harvested before the other plants need the space. Radishes can be mixed with seeds that are slow to germinate, such as parsnips. As they germinate, they will help to keep the soil from crusting over and mark the row for the parsnips. Usually it is the root of radish that is eaten, but the tender young leaves are also edible in salads.

Radishes likely originated in the Far East but their origin is shrouded in antiquity. They were grown by the Egyptians, Romans and Greeks before the birth of Christ. We tend to think of radishes as roundish, red vegetables to slice into a salad, but this type of radish did not evolve until the 16th century. Other cultures grow a wide assortment of radishes in various colors, sizes and forms. They can be black, white or red and 1/2 inch (1 cm) to 2 feet (60 cm) long—from the size of a pea to the size of a basketball. Radish is one of the largest crops of the greenhouse industry in Holland. They are exported to Germany where they are served with beer.

Radishes are fun for children to grow because the seeds are large, they germinate quickly and they can be harvested in as little as three weeks. There are many wonderful shapes and novelty radishes that are new on the market, including 'Purple Plum', 'Green Meat' and 'Red Meat'. Red Meat is green on the shoulder, white at the bottom and has a red center when it is mature.

Harvest Time: Radishes are harvested when the weather is cool—in the spring and again in the fall.

Height: 4 to 6 inches (10 to 15 cm).

Light and Soil: Radishes need to grow quickly and will do best in a fertile, well-drained soil that has had compost dug into it. In the spring they need full sun. During the height of the summer, they can be grown in light shade. The ideal pH is 5.8 to 7.8. If the longer varieties are grown, dig the soil deeply. Short varieties do well in containers.

How to Grow: Radish seeds are sown 1/2 inch (1 cm) deep and 1/2 inch (1 cm) apart. The rows should be 6 to 8 inches (15 to 20 cm) apart. Thin the radishes to 2 inches (5 cm). If they are not thinned they will not have the space or nutrients to properly form the root. Keep radishes well watered. They have shallow root systems and become pithy and hot-tasting if they dry out. To get a jump on the season, plant radishes in cold frames or under plastic in mid-February through March. Continue to sow them throughout the spring. They are more difficult to grow when the summers are hot, but they can be sown under the shade of the leaves of other crops or in a shaded part of the garden. Fall sowings should be made in late August.

Harvesting: Do not allow the roots to become too large. Harvest when they are 3/4 inch (2 cm) in diameter.

Storage: They are best eaten freshly picked, but they will keep in the refrigerator for at least a week. Cut off the leaves, which decompose quickly, and store the radishes in a plastic bag or container.

Problems: Cracking, pithiness, bolting and very hot radishes usually stem from stress due to too wet or too dry soils, or great fluctuations in soil moisture and heat.

Pests and Diseases: Radishes can fall victim to quite a few insect pests. The most annoying are flea beetles and cabbage maggots, which invade the root, making it inedible. If the radishes are harvested as soon as they are large enough to eat, there is less chance of the eggs having time to hatch. A cover of Reemay will protect the radishes from both insects. The slower-growing winter or Oriental radishes often have a problem with cabbage maggots.

Downy mildew may attack the late summer crop. For information on these problems, refer to chapter six, Pests and Diseases.

A soil-borne disease, **black root**, is sometimes a problem. Rotate the crop and only grow the small, round varieties that are less susceptible.

Varieties: 'Cherry Belle' and 'French Breakfast' are older varieties of round, red radishes that always do well in the garden. 'French Breakfast' seems to tolerate summer heat well. 'White Icicle' and 'Icicle Medium Top' are elongated, white, mild radishes that look like carrots. 'Scarlet Champion' and 'Champion' do well in the spring and fall.

RHUBARB *Rheum rhabarbarum*

Rhubarb is a perennial vegetable that is grown for its tart, red stalks. Planted in a site where it can remain undisturbed, rhubarb will continue producing with relatively little care for up to ten years. In the early spring it provides a fresh taste, in pies, cobblers or other cooked dishes. Later in the season, rhubarb mixed with strawberries makes a tasty pie or jam.

Rhubarb was originally grown for medicinal purposes and its cultivation dates back hundreds of years. It is likely a native of Siberia which has gradually been introduced around the world. Rhubarb is a vigorous plant that puts on a lot of growth each season, with large leaves that can be 18 inches (45 cm) in diameter. The stalks are red, or green tinged with red. The red-stalked varieties are superior; they are more tender and the red color is preferred. The leaves, which contain oxalic acid, are toxic, but it is safe to add them to the compost pile.

Harvest Time: The plants are harvested from April through July.

Height: 2 feet (60 cm).

Light and Soil: Plant rhubarb in a sunny spot with good drainage. Rhubarb has a deep root system and the soil should have compost and well-aged manure dug into it. Although rhubarb will grow in poorer soils, it will produce much better if it is planted in a well-prepared spot. The acid soils on the coast are fine for rhubarb, which does well with a ph of 5.5 to 7.0.

How to Grow: Rhubarb can be grown from seed, but that is a lengthy project. It is better to purchase a piece of root or an offshoot in the early spring. Rhubarb can also be planted in the fall if the roots are available, or if you are dividing a clump. Clumps can be divided by cutting the root with a sharp knife. When planting rhubarb, leave 3 feet (1 m) or more between clumps. The leaves are large and the plants take up a lot of room. Do not harvest the plants the first year and harvest lightly the second year. In the fall, after the plant has died back, clean up the old leaves and top-dress the site with compost, manure or other organic matter. In the spring, top-dress the plants with 6-8-6 and fertilize again in early July — rhubarb is a heavy feeder. The plants are fairly drought-tolerant because they have a deep root system, but do not totally ignore them during a dry summer.

When a stalk with flower buds forms, it should be removed so the plant uses its energy to produce shoots, instead of producing flowers.

Forcing is a technique that is not used much any more, but it is a way to have tender rhubarb shoots early in the spring. Before frozen foods and fruit from California were available year-round, forcing rhubarb was a way to have fruit out of season. The term "forcing" is often applied to bulbs that are brought into bloom by bringing them into a warm place during the winter. You can do the same thing with rhubarb but instead of flowers you are forcing the shoots. To force rhubarb, dig the crowns in the spring and plant them in damp sand or peat in a dark, warm room.

To produce tender pale shoots outside, place a bottomless, topless cup over the plant. The shoots grow tall to reach the light and produce tender stalks. When plants elongate and are pale from lack of chlorophyl, it is called etoliation.

Harvesting: Grasp the stem near the bottom and twist it off; this is preferable to cutting off the stalks. Remove the leaves. Always leave some shoots on the plant, as the leaves are needed to manufacture food for the plant to produce more shoots.

Stop harvesting most varieties by mid-July, although some can be harvested longer if they are producing nice tender stalks. Beware of overharvesting – the plant needs time to build up the root to produce next year's harvest. In any case, the stalks often become tough in the summer.

If the stalks have decreased in size, it is time to divide the root or harvest less if it is a young plant. As perennials age, there are fewer fibrous roots and the newer growth is to the outer part of the plant. Dividing the root rejuvenates the plant.

Storage: Rhubarb will keep one week wrapped in plastic in the refrigerator. The stalks can be cut up and frozen or used to make jam.

Pests and Diseases: Rhubarb is generally fairly free of problems. Remove diseased plants and do not replant rhubarb in the same spot.

Varieties: There is not usually much choice of variety in the garden centers and many are unnamed. 'Crimson' and 'MacDonald' are two good varieties for B.C.

RUTABAGA *Brassica napus*

Rutabaga, swede or Swedish turnip are some of the names this sturdy root goes under. The plants are cold-hardy and storage is simple– just leave them in the ground. The plants do well in our cooler maritime climate and they are very easy to grow. The flesh varies from white to yellow.

Rutabaga and turnips are similar in shape and are often confused, but they are two completely different species. The bigger, rougher-looking rutabaga takes a month longer than the turnip to mature, it is hardier, and it's stronger-flavored. It is thought that rutabaga is an unusual cross between turnip and cabbage that may have originated in Sweden during the Middle Ages.

Harvest Time: Fall through winter.

Height: 10 to 18 inches (25 to 45 cm).

Light and Soil: Rutabagas need a good soil with added organic matter, but avoid manure and lime unless clubroot is a problem in the garden. Rutabaga is susceptible to scab, so it is best to avoid areas where potatoes were grown the previous summer. They will grow in sun or light shade and do best with a pH of 6.0.
How to Grow: Rutabagas are direct-seeded mid-June to mid-July for a fall harvest; unlike turnips they require a long season. Sow the seeds 3/4 inch (2 cm) deep and thin the plants to 6 to 8 inches (15 to 20 cm) apart. Leave 16 inches (40 cm) between the rows. Fertilize with a basic fertilizer, 6-8-6, at sowing time. Rutabagas will benefit from mulching.
Harvesting: The sweetness of rutabagas will be enhanced by frost, and the large ones are just as good or better than the smaller ones. They range in size from about 4 to 8 inches (10 to 20 cm).
Storage: Leave them in the ground where possible. Otherwise they will keep for up to six months stored at 32°F (0°C).
Pests and Diseases: Cabbage maggot is the worst pest for rutabagas and they may be attacked by other kale pests and diseases, such as clubroot. see Chapter six, Pests and Diseases, for more information.

Rutabagas are also susceptible to **scab** and **Rhizoctonia rot**. Scab is just skin deep and it will not affect the crop's edibility. Avoid planting where potatoes have grown before and do not use lime where they are to grow that year. The rot fungus enters a wound, so control slugs, cutworms and maggots, and hoe with care. Do not store roots if they have spots on them.
Varieties: There are very few varieties available, but 'Alta Sweet' and 'Best of All' are good choices.

SPINACH *Spinacia oleracea*

Spinach is native to Iran and was not known elsewhere for many centuries. Gradually it was introduced by travelers through the Middle and Far East, reaching Spain via the Moors in the 1100s. Spinach is now universally grown, for use both as a cooked vegetable and as an ingredient in salads. The leaves are dark green, smooth or slightly crinkly and rich in vitamins.

Spinach is an annual and can germinate when the temperature is only 50°F (10' C). It grows best when the weather is cool and does very well on the West Coast. Freezing has fortunately eliminated the need to can spinach—a product edible only to Popeye.

New Zealand spinach (*Tetragonia tetragonioides*) is not a true spinach, because it is in a different family. Like spinach, its attractive triangular leaves are harvested one by one. It is a tender perennial that will withstand summer heat and makes a good spinach substitute, when common spinach is no longer available in midsummer. New Zealand spinach is a newcomer to our gardens, but it has been used for many years in both Australia and New Zealand. It is fast gaining many fans in North America. The tender young leaves are preferred to the older leaves, which have a strong flavor.

Harvest Time: Spinach is harvested in the late spring and early summer. It is harvested again in the fall through winter.

Height: 4 to 8 inches (10 to 20 cm).

Light and Soil: Spinach needs fertile soil that has had organic matter dug into it. During the summer it can tolerate shading, but for spring and fall plantings put it where it will get sun.

How to Grow: Spinach needs to grow quickly so the leaves will be lush and tender. Scatter 6-8-6 fertilizer before the seeds are sown. The seeds can be soaked for half an hour in lukewarm water before sowing, although I have sown seeds without soaking them with good results. Sow the seeds 1/2 inch (1 to 2 cm) deep and at 1-inch (2-cm) intervals. Thin the plants so they are 6 to 8 inches (15 to 20 cm) apart. New Zealand spinach is larger than spinach so give it more space–about 15 inches (38 cm) between plants. The thinnings can be used in salads; pull every other plant.

Plant spinach in beds rather than rows to maximize space. Do not allow the soil to dry out or the plants will bolt. Bolting is also caused by long summer days and warm weather. Some varieties are less susceptible to bolting.

In milder areas, covering the fall crop with Reemay will give some winter protection.

Harvesting: Larger, outer leaves can be removed one by one as needed or the whole plant can be harvested. The top 6 to 8 inches (15 to 20 cm) of New Zealand spinach can be harvested, which will help keep the rather bushy plant under control.

Storage: Eat spinach fresh from the garden or store it in a plastic bag in the refrigerator for up to a week. Spinach freezes well but should be blanched before freezing.

Pests and Diseases: The spinach grown at the U.B.C. Botanical Garden seems to overwinter well with no disease problems. Part of the success might be the raised beds, which have good drainage, and the generous spacing between the plants.

Insects that attack spinach are caterpillars, cutworms, slugs, and leaf miners. The primary disease problem is downy mildew. For tips on how to deal with these problems, consult chapter six, Pests and Diseases.
Varieties: The cold-resistant Savoy types, 'Bloomsdale Savoy' and 'Tyee' hybrids, are good choices to overwinter. 'Mazurka' F1 resists bolting when the warm weather arrives, making it a good choice for spring sowing.
Hint: Sow spinach in mid-September on the coast for an early harvest in March.

SQUASH, PUMPKIN and MARROW *Cucurbita pepo* (spaghetti squash, acorn squash, zucchini, marrows, pumpkin), C. *maxima* (many winter squash, Atlantic Giant-type pumpkin), C. *mixta* (winter squash, pumpkin) and C. *moschata* (butternut-type squash, pumpkin)

Pumpkins and squashes are members of the cucurbit, or cucumber, family, along with cucumbers and melons. All of the cucurbits are warm-weather crops. They are tropical vines that will die back with the first hard frost, although the mature fruit will withstand some frost. Squashes are the hardiest member of the cucurbits and they are varied in color, shape and size. Today we can grow very tiny pumpkins to mammoth pumpkins of contest fame. There are several species of pumpkin because we tend to call any squash that resembles a jack-o-lantern a pumpkin.

Squash and its close relatives are native to Mexico and South America and were introduced into Europe by explorers in the 1500s.

Squash is generally divided into two groups—summer and winter squashes. The only difference is those that are treated as summer squash—zucchini, patty pan types and crookneck—are eaten when they are small and the skin is thin. Winter squash—turban, marrows, butternut and acorn—are left on the vine until frost, when the skin has hardened and they can be stored for winter use. Summer squash, if it were allowed to mature, would also develop a hard skin that would allow it to be stored in the winter.

Squashes take up a lot of garden space and it is possible to have too much summer squash—remember all the jokes about the prolific zucchini—but two or more plants must be planted for pollination. For the average household, one or two summer squash plants per person and three or four winter squash are plenty.
Harvest Time: Summer squash are harvested from August through to

September and the winter squash from October through November.
Height: The vines sprawl in all directions but they hug the ground. The vines have tendrils and will climb if a fence or other object is in their path. Squash plants can be grown on a trellis, but the weight of the fruit will pull it off the vine, so nylon stockings or some other type of sling must be used to hold the fruit in place. Some varieties of squash are bush size, about 2 feet (60 cm) tall. These are ideal for small gardens and for containers.
Light and Soil: Squash seems to grow in most soils, but some added compost will not go amiss as it grows especially well in organic soils. The soil should be well drained and have a pH of 5.8 to 7.0. Plant squash in full sun.
How to Grow: Squash must not be planted out or sown until warm weather is assured. Raised beds, a sunny slope and soil covered with plastic will help get them into the ground earlier. If the seeds are sown the end of May to the first week in June, the ground does not need to be covered with plastic. Once the seeds are planted, try not to water until they have germinated, because water cools the soil. For the seeds to germinate, the soil temperature must be at least 63°F (16°C), and they will germinate with better success if the soil is even warmer.

Seeds can be started indoors in individual pots to be transplanted three to four weeks later. The best method for dealing with seeds is to presprout them between layers of damp paper towel placed in a plastic bag. Open the bag each day and check the seeds. Plant the sprouted seed when the root is just starting to show. Handle them with care; the emerging root can easily be damaged.

Mound soil up into a hill (this helps to warm up the soil) and plant three seeds per hill. The distance between hills will vary depending on the variety of squash or pumpkin, but about 4 feet (1.2 m) is average. If the weather turns cool when the plants are still small, cover them with a cloche to give them some protection.

Sprinkle a band of basic fertilizer like 6-8-6 around each plant when the seeds are sown or transplants put out. After six weeks, side-dress the plants with fertilizer. Squash are heavy feeders and they will grow very well in a compost pile. Occasionally they will self-sow from seed that has been dumped on the compost pile from kitchen refuse. The result will be a surprise, because squash plants freely hybridize and it would be impossible to know which squash were the parents.

Similar to cucumbers, the vines will set male flowers first and the female and more male flowers will follow later. Vines must grow a certain number of leaves before they will set flowers, so be patient. If you are using Reemay, remove it when the female flowers appear so that the bees can pollinate the flowers.

When the seeds are sown, keep the soil surface moist until the seedlings are growing. Once the plants are established, do not water from above—this can set the scene for diseases on the wet leaves. When you build the mounds, bury a plastic tube, about 2 inches (5 cm) in diameter, with one end in the soil at the bottom of the mound and the other end above the soil surface. You can then fill the tube with water, which will keep the root area moist. The plants need plenty of water once the fruit is set.

Pruning of squash and pumpkins seems to be a controversial subject. Some recommend pruning the vines once enough fruit has set. This has the advantage of limiting the space taken up by the vines, but the wound can be an invitation to disease and the extra leaves manufacture food for the plant. I do not prune the plants when I grow them, but it is a personal choice.

If you want to grow a giant pumpkin, start with the 'Atlantic Giant Pumpkin' seeds. Sow them indoors and plant them out when the soil warms up. Augment the soil with well-rotted manure and choose your sunniest spot. Once the plant has set one good fruit, remove all the others so that the vine is only supporting that one fruit. See that the plant is never under stress from lack of water or nutrients. Once the fruit has set, start a fertilizing program of 20-20-20, half-strength, once a week. It can be alternated with another fertilizer, such as 6-8-6.

Harvesting: Summer squash are harvested when they are big enough to use. Do not let the fruit get too large. If a fruit is missed, pick it off; large fruit left on the plant will cause the plant to stop producing. (Even large zucchini can be grated and used to bake wonderful cakes and loaves. If the kids object to the bits of green in the cake, peel the zucchini and they will never know!) Squash can be prickly to pick, but must be removed carefully so the vine is not injured. I prefer to use pruners and leave some stem on the fruit.

Winter squash and pumpkins are left until the frost. Once the vines die back, you will be surprised at just how much fruit there actually is under all those leaves. The exceptions are cool, wet summers, when there may not be enough sun to produce a sizable crop of winter squash. When the fruit is harvested, leave some stem for easier handling—and, of course, all good jack-o-lanterns need a stem.

Storage: Summer squash will keep in the refrigerator for two to three weeks. The larger summer squashes with tougher skins will keep several weeks in a cool place. If the squash has been left until the skin has hardened it can be stored like winter squash. Summer squash can be grated and frozen, or pickled.

Winter squash are cured at a warm temperature for three to four weeks until the skins are hard, then stored at 50 to 60°F (10 to 15°C). They will keep for four to nine months. This is one of the few vegetables that are not kept at near-freezing temperatures. Store them in a warm basement or even under the bed!

Pests and Diseases: Problem insects are cutworms, thrips and mites. For more information refer to chapter six, Pests and Diseases.

Squash can be attacked by powdery mildew, wilts and scab. See the Potato entry for information about scab.

Powdery mildew is probably the greatest problem on the coast, but it does not usually hit until August, when it covers the leaf surface and blocks photosynthesis. Avoid using areas of the garden that get a lot of morning mist or dew, and plant squash where there is plenty of air circulation. Some varieties are resistant to mildew.

Wilts are caused by several different diseases. If plants are affected pull them out and destroy them.

Varieties: 'Atlantic Giant' is the variety to grow if you want a huge pumpkin, but the vines take up a lot of room and you need a fork-lift truck or a couple of very strong people to move the pumpkin. 'Jack O'Lantern' is my favorite. It is the classic pumpkin and is tasty as well. 'Sweetie Pie' and 'Little Lantern' are miniatures that are decorative, as well as tasty when baked with a stuffing. 'Black Beauty' is a good zucchini and 'Sunburst' F1 is a bright yellow patty-pan squash that produces an abundance of fruit. 'Sweet Mama' was an All-American Selection some years ago and it is still a top variety. 'Vegetable Spaghetti' is a tasty, marrowlike squash that looks like thin spaghetti when it is scooped out after being cooked. 'Buttercup' is a turban-shaped squash with a good flavor. 'Hubbard Blue' is a large, blue gray squash about the size of a medium pumpkin. Try carving one instead of a pumpkin for an eerie look on Hallowe'en.

SWISS CHARD *Beta vulgaris*

Swiss chard is an all-season vegetable that is as ornamental as it is tasty. It is a member of the beet family but, unlike beets, it is tolerant of both heat and cold. Swiss chard is a biennial that forms a rosette of leaves in the first season, then elongates and blooms in the second year. If the plant blooms in the first season, it is called bolting, and it is usually the result of stress.

Swiss chard has been known since ancient times—it was gathered in the wild in the Mediterranean region. There were distinct varieties as far back as the time of Aristotle, who wrote about a red-stemmed variety—the strawberry chard of today. Swiss chard is related to beets but predates that vegetable by centuries.

Swiss chard is essentally a beet without the harvestable root. The leaves are sturdier and more upright than beets, and the stems are longer and thicker. The leaves are steamed and eaten as a vegetable or used in stir-fry dishes. Swiss chard leaves can also be substituted for cabbage in cabbage rolls.

Swiss chard will survive heavy harvesting and will send out more shoots so that you can continue to harvest the plants all through the summer and into the winter. If you have room for only one vegetable, this is the one to grow. It requires very little care for big returns.

Harvest Time: The stalks are harvested from spring through to the next spring, when the plants will bolt.

Height: 12 to 18 inches (30 to 45 cm).

Light and Soil: Swiss chard grows best planted in full sun, but will tolerate light shade. Although it will grow in most soils, the rewards are much greater if it is planted in rich garden soil that has had organic material added. Swiss chard does best when the pH is 5.8 to 7.0.

How to Grow: Sow the seeds in April through June. Sow seeds 3/4 inch (2 cm) deep and space the plants 12 inches (30 cm) apart. Like beets, the corky seeds are really several small fruits surrounded by a calyx and will usually have to be thinned. Sow double rows and stagger the spacing by alternating the plants in the rows to maximize the space. Leave 20 inches (50 cm) between the rows. Give the plants some basic fertilizer like 6-8-6 at sowing time and place a band of fertilizer beside the row during the growing season to keep new leaves coming. If production of leaves slows down, add fertilizer. The plants will benefit from being mulched—it conserves moisture and protects the roots during the winter.

Harvesting: You can begin harvesting once there are at least six good-sized leaves, picking two or three from each plant. As the plants mature, you can harvest more leaves at each picking. Twist the outer stems off at ground level, leaving the center leaves to continue growing. Twisting is better than using a knife to harvest; when you cut, it is impossible not to leave a stub that is an invitation to rot, diseases and pests.

Storage: Swiss chard will keep for a week in a plastic bag in the refrigerator. It can also be frozen, but on the coast it is not usually necessary—just leave it in the garden.

Pests and Diseases: Swiss chard is fairly free of pests and problems. The leaf miner can be a problem, but Swiss chard seems to be quite resistant, especially the white varieties. Their leaves are thicker and savoyed (wavy) which may make them less inviting for the miner. Refer to the Beets entry for more information on leaf miners.

Varieties: Rhubarb chard has bright red stalks and is an asset in the flower garden. When the sun shines through the crimson, translucent stems they are magnificent. 'Fordhook Giant' is the most cold-hardy and heat-resistant variety, with wide, white stalks that are ribbed like celery. The ruby or red chards do not tolerate the heat as well and tend to bolt. They are not as cold-hardy but will do well in milder winters.

TOMATO *Lycopersicon lycopersicum*

Tomatoes seem to be a favorite of gardeners. They are adaptable—growing in the greenhouse, containers, hanging baskets, or in the ground. There are many varieties, but here on the West Coast we generally do not have the heat needed to grow the really large beefsteak tomatoes. In fact, some years growing tomatoes at all becomes a victory, when a combination of cool nights and rainy days slows growth and promotes diseases.

Tomatoes are a warm-weather perennial, native to South America, but here they will not survive the frost and are grown as annuals. Tomatoes were cultivated by the Indians of South America and Mexico, where the forerunners of our present-day tomatoes still grow wild. When tomatoes arrived in Europe, it was thought they were poisonous because they are in the same family as the deadly nightshade. They have been called love apples, and the Italians called them golden apple, *pomo d'oro*.

Tomatoes come in many shapes and sizes and vary in color and sweetness. But everyone who has eaten home-grown tomatoes agrees that the flavor beats store-bought varieties. For commercial tomato growers, flavor is probably not at the top of the list of desirable characteristics; disease resistance, tough skins and size must take priority.

Harvest Time: The earlier varieties will be ready by midsummer, or earlier if they are started early, put in a cold frame and grown under

cloches when they are first set out in the garden. Tomatoes can be harvested as long as the weather, especially at night, stays warm.
Height: Tomatoes range in height from less than a foot (30 cm) to 6 feet (2 m) and over, depending on the variety. Some are very upright, while others like to sprawl. Tomatoes are classed as determinate or indeterminate. Determinate tomatoes are bush tomatoes, which reach a height of 1 to 2 feet (30 to 60 cm) and stop growing when the terminal bud sets fruit. The fruit ripens over a short period of time and these types are often field-grown commercially. The indeterminate varieties will continue to grow in height. They set fruit throughout the whole season, and as they grow they form fruit at each truss.
Light and Soil: The plants will need your warmest spot in the garden. An ideal spot is against a south-facing wall. They need full sun and good garden soil with compost added. Be careful not to give the plants too much nitrogen or they will put on a lot of leaf growth at the expense of the fruit. Tomatoes do best with a pH between 6.0 and 7.0. If you are adding lime use dolomite lime; it contains calcium, which helps prevent blossom end rot. Put the lime on the soil three weeks before setting out the transplants.
How to Grow: Tomatoes are most often started indoors and planted outside as transplants, although some varieties can be direct-sown. Sow the seeds indoors in a flat or individual pots in mid-March, and gradually pot them up into larger containers as they grow. A plant is ready for a larger pot when the roots have almost reached the bottom of the pot. To check, turn the pot upside down and tap the rim; the soil will come out intact if the roots are well formed. It is easy to see how close to the bottom the roots are growing. It is important not to hinder the growth by leaving the plants in too small a pot.

Tomato seeds need warmth to germinate—between 75 and 85°F (24 and 29°C). If you do not have heating cables, use the top of the refrigerator or any other warm spot for germination. A heating pad turned on low will also work. After the seeds germinate, they should be placed where they will get lots of light and kept at about 60°F (15°C). In May they can go into a cold frame if you have one, otherwise they must stay inside until they can go into the garden in June. Harden the plants off before they are planted out by giving them more sun each day.

To get a head start on the season, plants can be set out in the garden in May if they are covered with a cloche. If they are growing next to a wall, you can simply tack some plastic along the wall to cover the plants.

Wall-O-Water, a trade name for water-filled plastic tubes that are set around the plants, can also be used. The water absorbs heat during the day and releases it at night. It is important not to set unprotected plants out until the night temperature remains above 55°F (13°C). The cloches can be removed by the end of June or earlier if the plants have outstripped their enclosure and the nights are warm.

When the tomatoes are planted out, give them a balanced fertilizer like 6-8-6, placed in a circle 4 inches (10 cm) from the stem. I also mix some bone meal and a handful of wet peat moss into the bottom of the planting hole. Give the plants a liquid feed or side-dress them in mid-August.

The spacing of plants will depend on the variety. Those that need staking (indeterminate varieties) are usually spaced 2 feet (60 cm) apart and the bush varieties 2 to 3 feet (60 to 90 cm) apart.

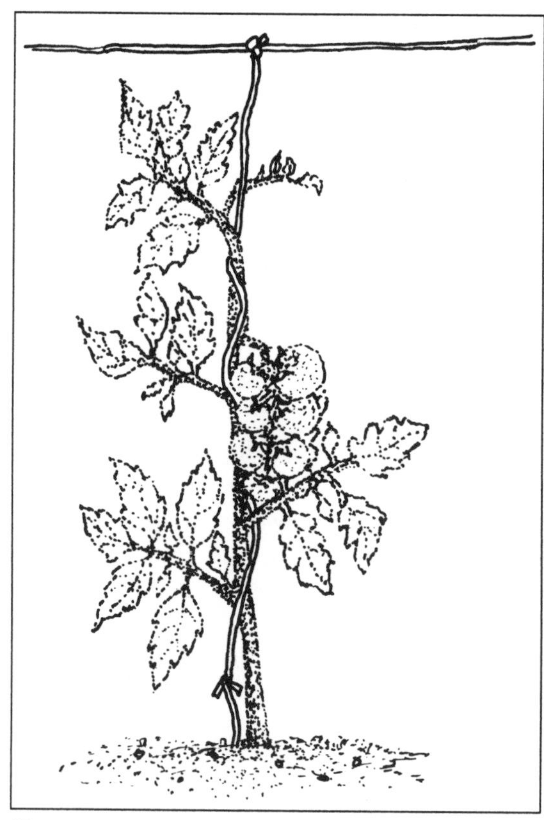

Tomatoes can easily be twined around a string instead of staking.

Most tomato plants, even the determinate varieties, need some staking in the garden. If you have unlimited space, the determinate varieties can be left to sprawl. The yield will be higher when the plants are allowed to sprawl, but slug damage and rotting of fruit that touches the soil can reduce the yield substantially. Tomatoes can be staked, grown inside wire cages or tomato hoops, or trained up string or mesh that is attached to the wall or onto overhead supports. I attach a string to the top of a sturdy stake or the wall if the plants are growing against the house. The bottom of the string is tied loosely around the base of the tomato stem and the stem is twisted around the string as the plant grows. Tomatoes need some help because, unlike peas or beans, they do not have tendrils or twine up a string naturally.

Indeterminate tomato varieties will need some pruning or they will become a jungle. Where each leaf joins the stem, a sucker (side shoot) will grow and become a large branch if it is left. Leave the main terminal shoot, which is the top of the plant where new growth originates, and two suckers at the bottom to continue growing; remove all the rest of the suckers. This will leave three strong shoots for each plant, which can be trained up three individual strings. If you prefer, one or two stems may be left rather than three. This sounds like a lot of pruning, but the suckers will be only 1 to 2 inches (2 to 5 cm) long and can be pinched off with your fingers. The plants need to be checked frequently for suckers; they put on a lot of growth quickly and it is amazing how fast a huge branch can grow. You can also thin some of the blossoms or tiny fruit on the determinate varieties to produce a better quality of fruit.

Do not remove what might seem to be excess leaves from tomato plants. The leaves manufacture food for the plant and shade the fruit, preventing it from becoming sun-burned. Keep the plants evenly watered and avoid extremes in soil moisture. Mulching helps tremendously during the summer.

By the end of August, some gardeners cut the tops back, on the theory that any fruit developing after that time will not have time to ripen. It is not always an advantage to remove the top—I prefer to remove excess blossoms or tiny fruit and leave the top to shade and make food for the plant.

In late summer, when the fruit is ripening, do not overwater the plants—the fruit will become watery and have less flavor. The stress also encourages the fruit to ripen. On the coast, where fall rains may make it impossible to control the water, try draping plastic over the supports to keep excess rain and heavy dew off the plants. The plastic will hasten ripening and help prevent diseases that are spread in the rain. It will also protect the plants from early frosts. The plastic should be lifted during the day when the sun is shining.

Tomatoes are a popular crop among those who have only a patio or balcony for growing. There are several small varieties that grow well in hanging baskets and the bush varieties do very well in containers. These plants will require more frequent fertilizing and watering than in-ground plants.

Harvesting: Tomatoes taste best if they are vine-ripened, but if frost threatens, pick the tomatoes and ripen them in a brown paper bag. Dark green fruit will never ripen, but light green tomatoes are wonderful sautéed in butter and they make the best pickles. The whole plant can be pulled in the fall and hung in a cool basement where the fruit will continue to ripen on the plant. If this is not possible, place the unripened fruit on trays in a cool place. If they are free of blemishes, they will continue to ripen over the next month.
Storage: Tomatoes will keep about a week when they are ripe and up to several weeks if they are green. Tomatoes may be made into juice, frozen, canned, dried or pickled. To freeze, place the fruit on trays, freeze, then store in plastic bags in the freezer. They must be used in cooked dishes; the skins will slip off as they are thawed. Green tomatoes can be used in pickles.
Problems: Tomato plants can be affected by many problems. Some are caused by disease or insects but many are cultural.

Poor fruit set—when the plants flower but no fruits form—is often the result of cool weather. Inadequate water can also reduce the fruit set, as well as very hot conditions (not usually a problem on the coast). Too much nitrogen can also cause a poor fruit set, since too much nitrogen causes excess leaf growth to the detriment of flowers. If the plants do not seem to be setting fruit, give them a slight shake to move the pollen around.

Leaf curl will occur if the plants have been heavily pruned or if they have had great fluctuations in watering. It is usually the older leaves that are affected and some varieties are more prone than others. It usually does not affect the plant unless it is caused by disease or herbicide damage rather than cultural conditions. Mulch the plants to keep the soil more evenly moist.

Blossom end rot affects tomatoes when the soil moisture level fluctuates from too dry to too wet—making calcium unavailable even when the soil has enough calcium. Mulch the plants for a more even distribution of moisture.

Cracking of the fruit happens if the soil is too wet or too dry. Some varieties are more prone to cracking. Mulch the plants.

Catfacing is a term used for misshapen fruit. It may be caused by cool weather during bloom or by herbicide damage.

Sunscald causes a whitish patch on the skin; in severe cases the area will become sunken. It happens when the fruit is suddenly exposed to the sun, usually during hot, dry weather. It can happen if the leaves are pruned or disease has damaged the leaves.

Abnormal growth is usually caused by herbicide damage. Tomatoes are very susceptible to 2,4-D injury, which causes twisted, thickened, narrow leaves and catfaced fruit. The stems will have many small bumps that are easily recognized as herbicide damage. You do not have to use herbicide on your tomatoes for them to be affected. Herbicide can drift quite a distance, or mulch from a treated lawn can cause the damage.

Pests and Diseases: Several insects attack tomatoes, including cutworms, caterpillars, flea beetles and whitefly. Whitefly is not usually a problem outside, but can be a real pest in the greenhouse.

Watch the plants when they are first put out and protect them from cutworms if they have been a problem in the garden. Flea beetles are cyclical; some years they can cause a lot of damage to small plants. Cover the seedlings with Reemay; once they put on some growth they can withstand most of the damage with no problem. Caterpillars, like flea beetles, are cyclical and may not be a pest most years. For more information on these pests, see chapter six, Pests and Diseases.

Tomato horn worm is not a problem on the coast but it is in the interior of the province. The adult is a furry, fast-flying moth. The large larva that does the damage is green, with white V-shaped markings on its sides and a black horn on its back end. There are two generations each summer. The larvae eat huge holes in the leaves, leaving large black pellets on the foliage and fruit. You can hand-pick them off the plants, but they are difficult to spot. Some gardeners have great success using a black light at night. It makes the caterpillar visible on the plants and they are easy to pick off.

Several fungus diseases may cause leaf and fruit spots. **Early blight** causes brown or black spots with noticeable concentric rings on the older leaves. The leaves will start to yellow and die prematurely, leaving the fruit unprotected from the sun. Damp rainy weather favors the disease, which can also affect the fruit. Early blight overwinters on old plants, so clean up the refuse in the fall. Keep plants growing vigorously, as the disease attacks weak plants.

Late blight affects both potatoes and tomatoes under certain conditions. Cool rainy weather with heavy dew favors the disease. It causes dark, water-soaked spots on the leaves and rotting of the fruit. To avoid late blight, water plants from beneath so that the foliage does not get wet; space the plants so there is good air circulation; and destroy potato culls and foliage. If late blight has been a problem in previous years, spray the plants at the beginning of August with copper spray, an organic fungicide. Spray more than one day before harvest and observe the waiting time before harvesting the fruit.

Virus diseases cause mottling, streaks and blotching of the leaves and fruit. If you smoke, avoid handling plants unless you wash your hands first, because tomatoes are very susceptible to a virus carried by tobacco. Keep garden refuse cleaned up, especially old potato and tomato plants, and rotate the tomato crop.

Varieties: There are many tomato varieties—more than any other vegetable. If I could only grow one, I would choose 'Sweet 100' but everyone has their own favorite. Two early tomato varieties developed at Oregon State University for the west coast are both determinate varieties: 'Oregon Spring' and 'Santiam'. They can be planted outside in mid-May. 'Celebrity' is a popular, tasty, determinate tomato, tolerant to many diseases. 'Early Cascade' F1 is a small tomato, 2 inches (5 cm), which ripens reliably on the coast. 'Fantastic' F1 is a good choice on the coast if you like the larger beefsteak-type tomatoes. Where the summers are hot, you can grow true beefsteak tomatoes, such as 'Ultra sweet' and 'Ultra Girl'. 'Sweet Chelsea Hybrid', 'Sweet Million', 'Sweet 100', and 'Sweetie' are staking cherry tomatoes that are very popular for their abundant, sweet-tasting fruit. 'Gold Nugget' is a yellow cherry tomato which contrasts nicely with the red varieties. 'Heinz 2653' is a canning variety that is pulpy rather than juicy like the types eaten fresh.

The letters given in some catalogues with the different varieties indicate resistance to disease and nematode damage (V—verticillium wilt, F—fusarium wilt, N—nematode).

Hint: Several gardeners have found that 'Sweet Million' tomatoes have some resistance to late blight. The plants eventually succumbed, but were harvested longer than other varieties.

TURNIP *Brassica rapa*

The vegetable that I called turnip when I was growing up in Winnipeg is called rutabaga (*B. napus*) on the coast, so I was a little startled with the results the first time I grew what I thought were turnips. The real turnip makes a lovely spring and summer vegetable. The tops are edible and the root is good raw or steamed. Turnips should be eaten as they mature because they do not keep well.

Turnips are native to Germany. They were brought to Canada in the

early 1500s by Jacques Cartier, the French explorer who discovered the St. Lawrence River.
Harvest Time: Harvest in the late spring through summer and again in the early fall. Unlike rutabagas, they will not withstand much of a frost.
Height: 10 to 18 inches (25 to 45 cm).
Light and Soil: Turnips require well-drained soil that has had compost dug into it (do not use fresh manure or the roots will fork). Plant turnips in full sun or light shade. The ideal pH is 6.0 to 8.0.
How to grow: Before seeding, rake some 6-8-6 into the soil. Turnips need to be grown quickly and eaten before they get too large – no more than 2 to 4 inches (5 to 10 cm) in diameter. Sow them fairly thickly in multiple rows and eat the thinnings for greens. (Turnip greens have a zip and are, perhaps, an acquired taste.) Eventually the plants should be spaced 4 inches (10 cm) apart. Make successive sowings. The plants grow quickly and some varieties will be harvested in a little over a month. Be sure they get adequate water while they are growing because they put on a lot of growth quickly. Turnips are a cool-weather crop and can be seeded mid-March through May. The plants do not do well in the heat, but mulching does help. For a fall harvest, make a final sowing at the beginning of August.
Harvesting: Turnips are ready for harvest when the root is 2 to 4 inches (5 to 10 cm) across. Do not let them get any larger.
Storage: Remove the tops and put them in a plastic bag in the refrigerator; they will keep for 10 days or more.
Problems: Woody roots are an indication that the plants were left too long before harvesting.
Pests and Diseases: They are fairly pest free, but can be subject to all the pests and diseases of the other kale crops: aphids, cutworms, slugs, beetles, root maggots and wireworms. Signs of clubroot or root maggots are wilting leaves (unless, of course, you forgot to water).
Varieties: 'Purple Top White Globe' are picture-perfect turnips with a reddish purple top. Pick them when they are about 3 inches (8 cm) across for a taste treat. 'Tokyo Cross' and 'Shogoin' have tender leaves, full of Vitamin A, that are tasty cooked when young.
Hint: Sow turnips in between slower-growing kale crops, such as cabbage and Brussels sprouts.

Quick Reference Chart

											Uses			Harvest Time							
	sun	tolerates light shade	lime	warm weather	cool weather	winter garden	direct seed	transplants	roots or tubers	# of days to germinate	fresh	frozen	pickled	spring	summer	fall	winter	usually pest free	perennial	ornamental	presprout
Asparagus	•	•			•		•		•	14	•	•		•				•	•	•	
Beans	•			•			•			7	•	•		•	•						•
Beets	•	•			•		•			10	•	•	•	•	•			•			
Broad Beans	•				•		•			7	•	•		•							
Broccoli	•	•	•		•	•	•	•		10	•	•		•	•	•					
Brussels Sprouts	•		•		•	•	•	•		10	•	•				•	•	•			
Cabbage	•	•	•		•	•	•	•		10	•		•	•	•	•	•				
Carrot	•	•			•		•			8	•	•	•		•	•	•				
Cauliflower	•	•	•		•	•	•	•		10	•	•	•	•	•	•	•				
Celery	•	•		•			•	•		21	•				•	•					
Corn	•			•			•	•		7	•	•			•	•					
Cucumber	•			•			•	•		7	•		•		•						•
Eggplant	•			•				•		14	•				•				•		
Endive	•	•			•		•	•		10	•			•		•					
Jerusalem Artichoke	•				•				•	–	•					•	•	•	•		
Kale	•	•	•		•	•	•	•		10		•			•	•	•	•		•	

Quick Reference Chart

	sun	tolerates light shade	lime	warm weather	cool weather	winter garden	direct seed	transplants	roots or tubers	# of days to germinate	Uses: fresh	Uses: frozen	Uses: pickled	Harvest Time: spring	Harvest Time: summer	Harvest Time: fall	Harvest Time: winter	usually pest free	perennial	ornamental	presprout
Kohlrabi	•	•	•		•		•	•		12	•	•			•	•		•			
Leeks	•	•			•	•	•	•		10	•					•	•	•			
Lettuce	•	•			•		•	•		7	•			•	•	•		•		•	
Melon	•			•				•		7	•				•	•		•			
Onion	•	•			•	•	•	•		10	•			•	•	•		•			
Parsnip	•	•			•		•			18	•					•	•	•			
Peas	•	•			•		•			7	•	•			•						•
Pepper	•			•				•		10	•	•			•	•		•		•	
Potato	•			•					•	14	•				•	•		•			•
Radish	•	•	•		•		•			7	•			•	•	•		•			
Rhubarb	•				•				•	–	•	•		•	•			•	•	•	
Rutabaga	•	•	•	•			•			10	•	•				•		•			
Spinach	•	•			•	•	•	•		8	•	•		•	•	•	•	•		•	
Squash	•			•			•	•		8	•	•			•	•		•			•
Swiss Chard	•	•			•	•	•	•		8	•				•	•	•	•		•	
Tomato	•			•				•		8	•	•			•	•					
Turnip	•	•	•		•		•			7	•	•		•	•	•		•			

Bibliography

All about Vegetables. Edited by Walter Doty. San Francisco: Chevron Chemical Co., 1980.

Bubel, Nancy. *The New Seed Starters Handbook*. Pennsylvania: Rodale Press, 1988.

Carr, Anna. *Color Handbook of Garden Insects*. Emmaus, Pa.: Rodale Press, 1979.

Colebrook, Binda. *Winter Gardening in the Pacific Northwest*. Seattle: Sasquatch Books, 1989.

Creasy, Rosalind. *The Gardener's Handbook of Edible Plants*. San Francisco: Sierra Club Books, 1986.

Crocket, James. *Crockett's Victory Garden*. Toronto: Little, Brown & Co. Canada, 1977.

Eldridge, Judith. *Cabbage or Cauliflower?* Boston: David R. Godine Publisher, 1984.

Faust, Joan. *The New York Times Book of Vegetable Gardening*. New York: The New York Times Book Company, 1975.

Gerber, H.S. *Major Insects and Allied Pests of Vegetables in British Columbia*. B.C. Ministry Of Agriculture and Food, 1983.

Harpstead, M.I.; Hole, F.D.; Bennett, W.F. *Soil Science Simplified*, 2nd

Ed. Iowa State University Press, 1988.

Hessayon, D. G. *The Vegetable Expert*. London: Britannic House, 1985.

How to Grow Vegetables and Berries. Sunset Books, Menlo Park, CA: Lane Publishing, 1982.

Hymans, E. *A History of Gardens and Gardening*. New York: Praeger, 1971.

MacNab, A.A.; Sherf, A.F.; Springer, J.K. *Identifying Diseases of Vegetables*. Pennsylvania: Pennsylvania State University, 1983.

Masefield, G.B.; Wallis, M.; Harrison, S.G.; Nicholson, B.E. *The Oxford Book of Food Plants*. London: Oxford University Press, 1971.

Newton, J.; Garland, M.; eds. *University of British Columbia Guide to Gardening in British Columbia*. Vancouver: U.B.C. Botanical Garden and Agricultural Sciences, 1990.

Solomon, Steve. *Growing Vegetables West of the Cascades*. Seattle: Sasquatch Books, 1989.

Tarrant, D. *A Year in Your Garden*. Vancouver: Whitecap Books, 1989.

Vegetables. Taylor's Guide, Boston: Houghton Miffin Company, 1987.

Ware, George W. *Complete Guide to Pest Control*. Box 9335, Fresno, California, 93791: Thomson Publications, 1980.

Wright, R. *The Story of Gardening*. New York: Dodd, Mead & Company, 1934.

Sources

These are just a few of the seed companies that supply vegetable seeds. You may find that you use just one company or you may use several companies for particular vegetables. There is no restriction on importing seeds for vegetables or flowers from the United States into Canada for use in the home garden.

Canada

A.J. Woodward & Sons, 635 Fort St., Victoria, B.C., V8W 1G1. They carry Sutton Seeds from England.

Alberta Nurseries & Seeds Ltd., Box 20, Bowden, Alta. T0M 0K0. Their catalogue lists seeds and perennials.

Alex Caron, RR 3, King City, Ont., L0G 1K0. Write to them for their potato price list.

Becker's Seed Potatoes, RR1, Trout Creek, Ont. P0H 2L0. Write to them for their list. They ship to Canada and the U.S.A.

C.A. Cruickshank, 1015 Mount Pleasant Rd., Toronto, Ont. M5M 2M1. They are representatives of Thompson & Morgan seeds in Canada.

Dill's Garden Giant, RR1 Windsor, N.S., B0N 2T0. Dill's sell giant pumpkin seeds.

Dominion Seed House, Georgetown, Ont. L7G 4A2. They carry a good selection of vegetable and flower seeds.

Gardener's Supply Co., 949 Wilson Ave., Thornhill, Ont. L3T 4A5. This company carries a wonderful collection of gardening accessories.

Island Seed Mail Order, Box 4278, St.A, Victoria, B.C., V8X 3X8. This company carries vegetables and herbs.

Lindberg Seeds Ltd., 803 Princess Ave. Brandon, Man., R7A 6N4. They carry vegetable seeds that would be suitable for colder areas of the country.

McFayden Seed Co., Box 1800 Brandon, Man., R7A 6N4. They carry vegetable seeds as well as gardening supplies.

Stokes Seeds, 39 James St., Box 10, St. Catherines, Ont. L2R 6R6. They carry an extensive vegetable and flower list.

T & T Seeds Ltd., Box 1710, Winnipeg, Man., R3C 3P6. This company carries vegetables, as well as herbs and flowers, that would be suitable for colder regions of the province.

Territorial Seed Co., Box 46225, Station G, 3760 W. 10th Ave. Vancouver, B.C., V6R 4G5. Territorial carries a wonderful selection of seeds specifically chosen for growing on the west coast. (See also U.S.A. address).

William Dam Seeds, Box 8400, Dundas, Ont. L9H 6M1. They carry untreated vegetable seeds.

United States

Abundant Life Seed Foundation, Box 772, 1029 Lawrence St., Port Townsend, WA, 98368. A nonprofit corporation that carries vegetable seed.

Burpee, 300 Park Ave., Warminster, PA, 18974. They carry a large variety of seed (U.S.A. only).

Gardener's Supply, 128 Intervale Rd., Burlington VT, 05401. A good garden supply company (U.S.A. only).

Heirloom Garden Seeds, Box 138, Guerneville, CA, 95446. They carry heirloom vegetable varieties.

Johnny's Selected Seeds, Foss Hill Rd., Albion, ME, 04910. They are well known for their vegetables.

Stokes Seed, Box 548, Buffalo, New York, N.Y. 14240. Stokes carries a good selection of vegetable and flower seed.

Territorial Seeds, Box 27, Lorane, OR, 97451. They carry a selection of seeds that do well on the west coast (see also Canadian address).

Thompson and Morgan, Box 1308, Jackson, NJ, 08527. They carry a good selection of vegetable seed and are known for their wide selection of flower seed.

Tilinghast Seed, Box 738, La Conner, WA, 98257. This seed house was established in 1885. They carry vegetable seed and have a wonderful store to visit in La Conner.

Index

Pages given in boldface indicate main entries.

Judy Newton has been gardening for most of her life, in climates as diverse as Winnipeg, Vancouver and California. In 1988 she formalized this interest with a degree in Plant Science from the University of British Columbia. She now holds the position of Education Assistant at the U.B.C. Botanical Garden, where she arranges and teaches classes, conducts tours and answers public inquiries.

Her writing has appeared in several West Coast publications. She writes a monthly column for *Gardens West*, as well as regular feature articles. She authored *Hortline Questions and Answers*, published by the U.B.C. Botanical Garden, and was the technical coordinator, editor and one of several authors of the *U.B.C. Guide to Gardening in British Columbia*, published in 1990. This is her first full-length book.

She has recently given up her large yard and garden for a townhouse, where she is enjoying the challenge of gardening in containers.